fresh food favorites

microwave cooking library®

by barbara methven

microwave cooking library®

Fresh produce not only improves the flavor and variety of our meals, it contributes to good health by providing fiber, vitamins, minerals and cancer-fighting enzymes. Adding more fresh foods to your diet is easy and enjoyable when you take advantage of seasonal diversity.

During your local growing season, farmers' markets introduce an exciting variety of fresh produce. And, thanks to an international shipping network, fresh foods from other areas are available at their peak of quality year-round at your supermarket.

Fresh Food Favorites offers you quick and easy recipes that enhance the flavor of fresh foods at their seasonal best. Cooking techniques include conventional methods, when these are best suited to the quality or style of a dish, and microwaving, to retain flavor, crispness and color.

Barbara Methven

Barbara Methven

CREDITS:
Design & Production: Cy DeCosse Incorporated
Art Director: Mark Jacobson
Test Kitchen Supervisor: Ellen Meis
Project Manager: Marcia Chambers
Home Economists: Virginia A. Hoeschen, Ellen Meis, Peggy Ramette
Dietitian: Hill Nutrition Associates, Inc.
Consultants: Beatrice Ojakangas, Peggy Ramette, Grace Wells
Editor: Janice Cauley
Director of Development Planning & Production: Jim Bindas
Production Manager: Amelia Merz
Electronic Publishing Specialist: Joe Fahey
Production Staff: Stephanie Beck, Adam Esco, Melissa Grabanski, Eva Hanson, Mike Hehner, Robert Powers, Mike Schauer, Nik Wogstad
Studio Managers: Mike Parker, Cathleen Shannon
Assistant Studio Manager: Rena Tassone
Lead Photographer: John Lauenstein
Photographers: Rebecca Hawthorne, Rex Irmen, Bill Lindner, Mark Macemon, Paul Najlis, Chuck Nields, Mike Parker
Contributing Photographer: Phil Aarestad
Food Stylists: Nancy J. Johnson, Abigail Wyckoff
Printed on American paper by: R. R. Donnelley & Sons (0593)

CY DE COSSE INCORPORATED
Chairman: Cy DeCosse
President: James B. Maus
Executive Vice President: William B. Jones

Library of Congress Cataloging-in-Publication Data

Methven, Barbara.
 Fresh food favorites / by Barbara Methven.

 p. cm. — (Microwave cooking library)
Includes index.
ISBN 0-86573-538-7

 1. Cookery (Fruit) 2. Cookery (Vegetables) I. Title. II. Series.
TX811.M48 1993
641.6'4 — dc20   92-43040

Additional volumes in the Microwave Cooking Library series are available from the publisher:

• Basic Microwaving
• Recipe Conversion for Microwave
• Microwaving Meats
• Microwave Baking & Desserts
• Microwaving Meals in 30 Minutes
• Microwaving on a Diet
• Microwaving Fruits & Vegetables
• Microwaving Convenience Foods

• Microwaving for Holidays & Parties
• Microwaving for One & Two
• The Microwave & Freezer
• 101 Microwaving Secrets
• Microwaving Light & Healthy
• Microwaving Poultry & Seafood
• Microwaving America's Favorites
• Microwaving Fast & Easy Main Dishes

• More Microwaving Secrets
• Microwaving Light Meals & Snacks
• Holiday Microwave Ideas
• Easy Microwave Menus
• Low-fat Microwave Meals
• Cool Quick Summer Microwaving
• Ground Beef Microwave Meals
• Microwave Speed Meals

• One Pound of Imagination: Main Dishes
• One-dish Meals
• Light Meals with Meat
• 100 Ideas for Today's Chicken

Contents

What You Need to Know Before You Start

America is rediscovering fruits and vegetables. Thanks to an excellent shipping system, even residents of the most northern areas can enjoy some form of fresh produce year-round. We experiment with the unfamiliar and become re-acquainted with "exotics" our great-grandmothers considered staples of the home garden. We no longer believe bigger is better; we appreciate young, tender and tasty baby vegetables.

All produce, whether shipped in or home-grown, is at its best during its peak season. In the summer, frequenters of roadside stands and farmers' markets find not only bargains but locally grown fresh fruits and vegetables at the peak of perfection. Some less familiar varieties may not be grown in sufficient quantities to stock the supermarkets, but they can provide an exciting culinary experience.

Fighting Disease with Food

We've always known that vegetables are good for you, but nutritional research shows just how good that can be. Some people are less susceptible to heart disease or some cancers because of their diet. Fiber plays an essential part in a healthy diet. Fresh fruits and vegetables, especially those eaten with their skins on, are a major source of fiber.

Cruciferous vegetables produce enzymes that may break down cancer-producing chemicals. Most of these are in the cabbage family, but also include watercress, arugula, kale, collards and mustard and turnip greens. The American Cancer Society recommends serving these vegetables several times a week as a protection against some cancers.

Reduced risk of some cancers has also been linked to beta-carotene and vitamin C. The cabbage family rates high in this respect, too, as do dark green, leafy vegetables like spinach, romaine, endive, chicory and escarole. To vary the menu, include vitamin C rich asparagus, green and red peppers, green beans, bean sprouts, onions, okra, summer squashes and tomatoes. Other sources of beta-carotene and vitamin C are yellow-orange vegetables (carrots, sweet potatoes, winter squashes) and yellow-orange or red fruits (apricots, berries, cantaloupes, cherries, papayas, peaches, pineapples, plums, watermelons). All citrus fruits and their juices supply vitamin C.

How to Use This Book

These recipes focus on freshness. Unless otherwise stated, all vegetables and fruits used are fresh. The ingredient lists for the recipes specify fresh or dried herbs. Generally, one tablespoon of chopped fresh herbs equals one teaspoon of dried herbs.

Nutritional Information

Per serving nutritional values and diabetic exchanges follow each recipe. When a recipe serves four to six persons, the analysis applies to the greater number of servings. In the case of alternate ingredients, the analysis applies to the first ingredient listed. Optional ingredients are not included in the analysis.

Prior to freezing, blanch fresh vegetables by plunging them in boiling water until color brightens.

Immediately transfer vegetables to ice water to stop the cooking process. Blanching stops maturation and preserves freshness.

Storing Fresh Produce

The keeping quality of fresh fruits and vegetables varies greatly. Winter squash will keep for months if stored in a cool, dry place. Other vegetables, like corn and beans, should be cooked as soon as possible after picking. An enzyme in these vegetables causes them to continue to mature until the process is stopped by blanching or cooking.

Tomatoes will not ripen after they have been chilled, so store them at room temperature until fully ripe. Peaches, nectarines and melons may also need some time at room temperature to soften. Pears taste best if picked early and allowed to ripen off the tree in a loosely closed paper bag. Check them frequently at the stem end, as they can ripen along the core before the outside seems soft. Asian pears keep exceptionally well — up to three months in the refrigerator.

Fruits that don't continue to ripen after harvesting, such as berries, must be picked ripe for peak flavor and sweetness and then handled delicately.

Raspberries are particularly vulnerable to damage. Layer unwashed berries on paper towels in a large plastic container and refrigerate until ready to use. If you freeze berries when they are plentiful for later use in recipes calling for fresh fruit, remember that frozen berries exude moisture as they defrost. You will need to adjust the recipes to allow for a greater amount of liquid.

Most apples keep well. Some delightful regional varieties appear in local markets for a limited time in the fall, but those that do not ship well may be unknown outside their home territory. If you don't know whether an apple is best for eating raw, cooking or all-purpose use, ask the seller.

Most fruits and vegetables should not be washed until preparation time. Moisture promotes decay, although some humidity inside the storage container is desirable. If you shop at a market that sprays vegetables with water for display, dry them well before storage. Inside the refrigerator, keep produce in a crisper or a perforated plastic bag.

Produce Identification Guide

Pictures on the following pages will help you recognize different forms of produce when you find them in the market. The items pictured are generally available nationwide and do not include local varieties that are not shipped outside their regions.

Asparagus and Artichokes. Choose tightly closed buds. Flowering on asparagus and open petals on artichokes indicate overmaturity.

Celery, Celery Root and Fennel. Celery adds flavor to both hot and cold dishes. Choose small celery roots and blanch peeled slices in acidulated water (water with lemon juice or vinegar added). Fennel's anise-flavored bulb complements shellfish, chicken or pork.

Cabbage Family. These vegetables, which are rich in vitamins A and C, belong to the cruciferous group. Choose firm heads that feel heavy for their size. Store them unwashed in perforated plastic bags for up to 1 week.

Okra, Cucumbers and Eggplants. Cook small, whole okra briefly. Cutting okra pods or long cooking releases a sticky sap, used to thicken gumbos and stews. Most commercially grown cucumbers are waxed for longer shipping life and should be peeled before use. Choose firm, shiny eggplant.

Cooking Greens. Select brightly colored, crisp leaves and store them unwashed in perforated plastic bags. Greens are exceptionally low in calories and rich in vitamins A and C. Serve spinach and tangy sorrel as cooked vegetables or salad greens. Use both greens and stems of Swiss chard. Cook the stems a few moments before adding the leaves.

Salad Greens. When making salads, be sure to include dark-colored leaves, which are richest in vitamins and minerals. Some markets provide salad mixtures that combine colors and textures and balance buttery and piquant lettuces. For tang, try endive, escarole or radicchio in salads or braised in butter. To barbecue greens for a salad, halve radicchio or Belgian endive, brush with vinaigrette and brown lightly over slow coals.

Mushrooms. In addition to the familiar button mushrooms, growers now cultivate several types distinctive both in shape and flavor. Delicate enokis should be eaten raw or only briefly cooked. Smooth-fleshed oysters are subtly flavored. Crimini (brown) mushrooms resemble buttons but taste sweeter. Meaty shiitakis have a rich, earthy flavor. Morels are highly prized, rich-flavored mushrooms and appear in the markets occasionally.

New and Unusual Vegetables. Among new varieties are *lettich,* a salad green developed from romaine and spinach, and *broccoflower,* which combines the color of broccoli with the form and flavor of cauliflower. Purple potatoes and yellow beets offer color. Elegant French beans and white eggplants have a long history but are new to American markets. For the ultimate garnish, choose an ornamental bouquet of baby vegetables, lightly steamed to preserve their color, texture and delicate flavor.

Onions. Several types of white, yellow and red onions, harvested and dried in the fall, are available year-round. In early summer, look at farmers' markets for mild locally grown onions, which have a short storage life due to their juiciness. Walla Walla and Vidalia onions have an exceptionally sweet flavor because of the soils in which they grow. Leeks demand careful cleaning, but are well worth the effort, both as a side dish and in soups or stews.

Beans, Peas and Corn. Snap beans should be blanched or cooked as soon as purchased. Beans continue to mature even under refrigeration. Fresh shelled beans, like lima or fava, are the fresh form of beans that are commonly dried. Shell English peas just before cooking. Snow peas are edible pods, while sugar snap peas combine a tender edible pod and plump peas. Corn on the cob, cooked the day it is picked, provides one of summer's delights.

Peppers. Green bell peppers ripen to red if left on the vine to mature. Red, yellow and orange bells may be cooked, but use purple peppers raw to retain color. Pimientos are smaller and more tapered than bells. Light green Gypsy peppers resemble mild chilies, but taste sweet. Chilies range from mild (ancho, poblano) to hot (jalapeño, serrano). Usually, the smaller the pepper, the more fiery the flavor. Removing seeds and ribs lessens the heat.

Potatoes. Choose thick-skinned, mealy russet potatoes for baking. Boil or steam thin-skinned, waxy types, such as long red, round red or white, and new potatoes. Store potatoes unwashed in a cool, dry, dark place. Dry-fleshed sweet potatoes have tan skins, golden flesh and mealy texture. They are less sweet than the moist, red variety, often called yams.

Root Vegetables. Leave roots, skin and 1 to 2 inches of the stem on beets during cooking to prevent bleeding. To preserve the delicate, oyster-like flavor of salsify, cook it in acidulated water on the day you buy it. Jícama, either raw or cooked, has a taste and texture similar to water chestnut. Turnips are more delicate in flavor when young, while a rutabaga's flavor strengthens as it matures. For a sweet parsnip, select small to medium roots after the first frost.

Summer Squash. Although summer squashes are most plentiful in summer, they are available year-round. They should be harvested when young and immature, while their seeds and skins are still tender and edible. For the best flavor, look for zucchini and yellow squash that are 4 to 6 inches long. If you can find them, try baby zucchini with the blossoms still attached. Serve summer squash raw or cooked just until tender-crisp. The chayote is a tropical squash with one seed that is edible and nutty-flavored when cooked. Cut right through the seed as you slice the chayote.

Winter Squash. These mature squashes are harvested in the fall after their thick rinds have hardened. Uncut, they keep well in a cool, dark place. Cut large squash, like pumpkin, hubbard and banana, in serving-size pieces before cooking. The others should be rinsed, halved and seeded before cooking, except spaghetti squash. Pierce the shell of this squash in several places to allow steam to escape, then microwave it whole. After cooking, cut the squash, scoop out the seeds and remove the spaghettilike strands with a fork.

Tomatoes. The best time to feast on tomatoes is when home-grown varieties appear in gardens, markets and roadside stands. Out of season, try locally grown hothouse tomatoes, which can be kept at room temperature to ripen. Tomatoes that have been picked early for safe shipping or chilled before they are fully ripe never achieve true tomato flavor. Roma (plum) tomatoes have thicker skins and withstand shipping well, so they can be allowed to ripen longer before harvesting. Tomatillos resemble green tomatoes in flavor. Use them raw in salads or cooked for salsas.

Fresh Herbs. Fragrant herbs enhance the flavor of foods. Most are at their best when young and fresh, although oregano's flavor improves with drying. Many supermarkets carry fresh herbs all year. During the growing season, farmers' markets provide large bouquets at a small cost, so you can use them lavishly as a garnish or basting brush, or lay them over coals to perfume the smoke when grilling.

Apples and Pears. Choose apples to suit your purpose. Cooking apples keep their shape when baked. Eating apples are crisp and juicy when raw. All-purpose apples satisfy either use. Pears, except Asian pears, are one of the few fruits that ripen and develop flavor after picking.

Berries and Cherries. Most ripe berries are fragile and naturally sweet. Tart, durable cranberries and currants must be cooked and sweetened. Several varieties of sweet eating cherries are available in supermarkets. Farmers' stalls sometimes supply sour pie cherries for cooking.

Citrus Fruits. Supplies of most citrus fruits peak in winter. For juiciness, choose fruits that are heavy for their size, with thin, smooth skins.

Tropical or Exotic/Unusual Fruits. Select these fruits for a festive dessert, salad or garnish. Unusual flavor or exotic appearance makes tropical fruits a treat for special occasions.

Familiar Tropical Fruits. Plantains and avocados are used as vegetables. Bananas continue to ripen and develop flavor at room temperature. Pineapples soften, but will not ripen after harvesting.

Grapes and Figs. For sweetness and flavor, choose grapes with fully developed color that are fairly soft to the touch but firmly attached to their stems. Figs must be tree ripened, so fresh figs are highly perishable and in limited supply outside their growing area.

Melons. Generally, melons weighing over 5 pounds have fuller flavor than smaller ones. Keep whole melons at room temperature until fully ripe. Refrigerate cut melons but, to preserve moisture, don't scoop out the seeds until ready to use.

Peaches, Plums and Apricots. Although they soften to a ripe texture at room temperature, these fruits do not develop flavor after picking. When selecting peaches, nectarines and apricots, look for fragrant fruit with a strong golden color behind the blush. Ripe plums yield to gentle pressure on the tip.

Rhubarb. Select firm, crisp stalks with bright green, pink or red color. Discard the leaves, which can be toxic.

Asparagus and Artichokes: a) Asparagus b) Artichoke

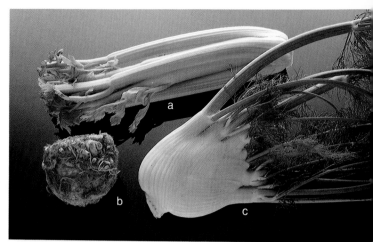

Celery, Celery Root and Fennel: a) Celery b) Celery Root c) Fennel

Cabbage Family: a) Bok Choy b) Red Cabbage c) Broccoli d) Cauliflower e) Savoy Cabbage f) Brussels Sprouts g) Kohlrabi h) Green Cabbage

Okra, Cucumbers and Eggplants: a) Okra b) Cucumbers c) Eggplant

9

Cooking Greens: a) Collards b) Kale c) Swiss Chard d) Turnip e) Mustard f) Beet
g) Spinach h) Sorrel

Mushrooms: a) Enoki b) Shiitake c) Crimini (Brown) d) Morel e) White Button f) Wood-ear
g) Chanterelle h) Oyster

Salad Greens: a) Escarole b) Chicory (Curly Endive) c) Romaine Lettuce d) Red Leaf Lettuce e) Limestone Lettuce f) Iceberg Lettuce g) Green Leaf Lettuce h) Boston Lettuce i) Watercress j) Belgian Endive k) Oak Leaf Lettuce l) Radicchio m) Arugula (Rocket)

New and Unusual Vegetables: a) Yellow Beets b) Lettich c) Baby Carrots d) Broccoflower e) Baby Zucchini f) Japanese Eggplant g) Tiny New Potatoes h) Baby Patty Pan and Sunburst Squashes i) French Beans j) White Eggplant

Onions: a) Leek b) Red c) Green (Scallions) d) Vidalia e) Yellow f) Chives g) Garlic
h) Walla Walla i) White j) Shallot k) Yellow, White and Red Pearl

Beans, Peas and Corn: a) Green Beans b) Corn c) Chinese Long Beans d) Snow Pea Pods
e) Fava Bean f) English Pea g) Sugar Snap Peas h) Yellow Wax Bean i) Italian Green Beans

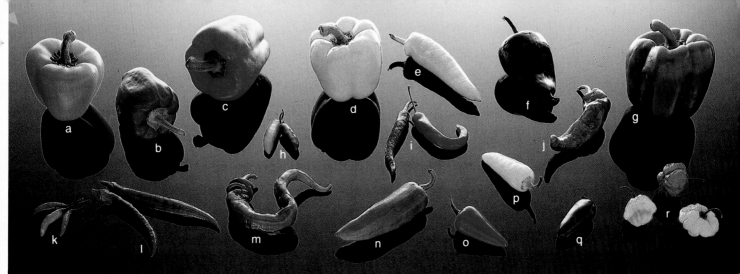

Peppers: a) Orange Bell b) Purple Bell c) Red Bell d) Yellow Bell e) Hungarian Yellow Wax
f) Poblano g) Green Bell h) Serranos i) Green and Red Chilies j) Nambe k) Miniature Chilies
l) Calientes m) Grinch Finger n) Green Anaheim o) Red Fresno p) Yellow Wax q) Jalapeño
r) Scotch Bonnets

Potatoes: a) Round White b) Russet c) Round Red d) Sweet (dry-fleshed) e) Sweet (moist-fleshed)

Root Vegetables: a) Turnips b) Radishes c) Jícama d) Carrots e) Rutabaga f) White Radishes
g) Parsnips h) Red Beets

Summer Squash: a) Zucchini b) Scallopini c) Sunburst d) Yellow Zucchini e) Chayote
f) Patty Pan g) Yellow Crookneck

Winter Squash: a) Hubbard b) Acorn c) Delicata d) Turban e) Buttercup f) Butternut
g) Spaghetti h) Sweet Dumpling i) Pumpkin

Tomatoes: a) Round Reds b) Tomatillos c) Yellow Pears d) Red Pears e) Yellow Round
f) Red Cherries g) Yellow Cherries h) Red Romas (Plum)

Fresh Herbs: a) Basil b) Italian Parsley c) Parsley d) Mint e) Rosemary f) Dill g) Oregano
h) Fennel i) Thyme j) Cilantro k) Sage l) Chervil m) Marjoram n) Tarragon

Apples and Pears: a) Red Delicious b) Golden Delicious c) Jonathan d) Rome Beauty e) Fireside
f) McIntosh g) Cortland h) Granny Smith i) Gala j) Seckel k) Bosc l) Forelle m) Asian Pear
n) Comice o) Red Bartlett p) Bartlett q) Star Crimson r) d'Anjou

Berries and Cherries: a) Red and Black Raspberries b) Strawberry c) Lambert Cherries
d) Rainier Cherries e) Blackberries f) Cranberries g) Blueberries h) Currants

Citrus Fruits: a) Red Grapefruit   b) Lemon   c) Mandarin Oranges   d) Navel Orange
e) Juice Orange   f) Tangerines   g) Lime   h) Grapefruit

Tropical or Exotic/Unusual Fruits: a) Passion Fruit   b) Pomegranate   c) Carambolas (Star Fruit)
d) Mangos   e) Kiwifruit   f) Pepinos   g) Yellow Tamarillos   h) Papaya   i) Feijoas   j) Red Tamarillos

Familiar Tropical Fruits: a) Red Bananas b) Pineapple c) Avocados d) Plantains e) Bananas

Grapes and Figs: a) Green Seedless Grapes b) Kadota Figs c) Red Seedless Grapes
d) Champagne Grapes e) Black Mission Figs

Melons: a) Watermelon b) Seedless Watermelon c) Yellow Watermelon d) Cantaloupe
e) Honeydew f) Casaba g) Crenshaw h) Santa Claus

Peaches, Plums and Apricots: a) Nectarines
b) Peach c) Italian Prune Plums d) Black
Plum e) Red Plum f) Apricots

Rhubarb: Red

Fresh Beverage Ideas

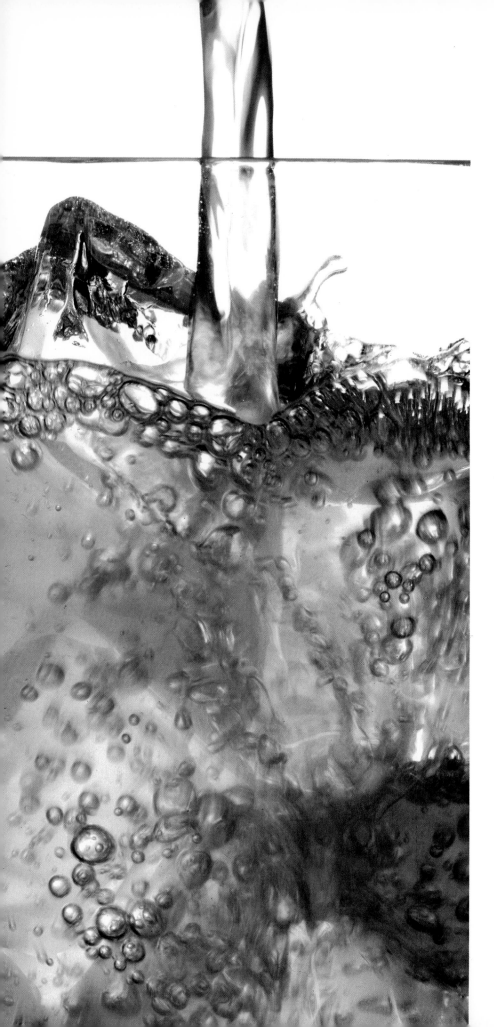

Fresh Ginger Ale

  6 cups hot water, divided
  3 tablespoons grated fresh
      gingerroot
½ teaspoon white
      peppercorns
½ cup honey
½ cup sugar
  1 cup lemon juice, strained
¾ cup orange juice, strained

8 servings

In 4-cup measure, combine 2 cups water, the gingerroot and peppercorns. Cover with plastic wrap. Microwave at High for 5 to 6 minutes, or just until boiling. Let stand, covered, for 5 minutes. Strain mixture through cheesecloth-lined strainer into 8-cup measure. Set liquid aside.

Return gingerroot and peppercorns to 4-cup measure. Add 2 cups water. Stir to combine. Cover with plastic wrap. Microwave at High for 5 to 6 minutes, or just until boiling. Let stand, covered, for 5 minutes. Strain liquid into reserved liquid. Set aside. Discard gingerroot and peppercorns.

Place remaining 2 cups water in 4-cup measure. Microwave at High for 4 to 5 minutes, or until boiling. Add honey and sugar. Stir until sugar is dissolved. Cool slightly. Add mixture to reserved liquid. Stir in juices. Serve warm, or chill and serve over ice. Mix equal parts fresh ginger ale and chilled carbonated water, if desired.

Per Serving: Calories: 130 • Protein: 0
• Carbohydrate: 35 g. • Fat: 0
• Cholesterol: 0 • Sodium: 8 mg.
Exchanges: 2¼ fruit

Iced Strawberry Tea

2 cups whole strawberries,
  hulled
1/2 cup hot water
1/4 cup sugar
9 cups prepared iced tea

9 servings

Place strawberries in 1 1/2-quart casserole. Cover. Microwave at High for 3 to 5 minutes, or until hot, stirring once. Strain berries through fine-mesh strainer into large mixing bowl, pressing with back of spoon to release juice. Discard pulp and seeds. Strain juice through cheesecloth-lined strainer into 4-cup measure. Set juice aside.

In 2-cup measure, combine water and sugar. Stir until sugar is dissolved. Stir mixture into strawberry juice. Pack tall serving glasses with ice. Add 2 tablespoons strawberry mixture and 1 cup iced tea to each glass. Mix well. Garnish each serving with additional whole strawberries, if desired.

Per Serving: Calories: 34 • Protein: 0
• Carbohydrate: 9 g. • Fat: 0
• Cholesterol: 0 • Sodium: 7 mg.
Exchanges: 1/2 fruit

Green Apple-Mint Ice Cubes with Soda ▲

2 medium green cooking
  apples, cored and thinly
  sliced
1/4 cup lemon juice
3 cups hot water
1/2 cup sugar
32 small fresh mint leaves
  Chilled carbonated water,
  lemon-lime soda or mineral
  water

8 servings

In 3-quart casserole, combine apples and juice. Toss to coat. Set aside. In 8-cup measure, combine water and sugar. Stir until sugar is dissolved. Cover with plastic wrap. Microwave at High for 7 to 10 minutes, or until boiling. Pour hot mixture over apples. Cover. Let stand for 1 hour, stirring once or twice.

Strain mixture through fine-mesh strainer into 8-cup measure, pressing with back of spoon to remove excess moisture. Discard apple slices. Place 1 mint leaf in each section of two 16-cube ice cube trays. Pour juice evenly into trays. Freeze at least 3 hours.

Pack serving glasses with 4 cubes each. Add whole strawberries, apple slices or wedges of pineapple or orange, if desired. Pour carbonated water over cubes.

Per Serving: Calories: 85 • Protein: 0 • Carbohydrate: 22 g. • Fat: 0
• Cholesterol: 0 • Sodium: 2 mg.
Exchanges: 1 1/2 fruit

Orange Tea Slush

  4 cups hot water
  ½ to 1 cup sugar
  2 tablespoons loose black tea leaves
  1 tablespoon grated orange peel
    Orange-flavored liqueur (optional)

4 servings

In 8-cup measure, combine water and sugar. Stir until sugar is dissolved. Microwave at High for 9 to 15 minutes, or until boiling. Stir in tea leaves and peel. Cover with plastic wrap. Let stand for 5 minutes.

Strain mixture through cheesecloth-lined strainer into 11 x 7-inch baking dish, pressing with back of spoon to remove excess moisture. Discard tea leaves and peel. Cool tea slightly. Freeze 2 hours, or until firm, stirring every 30 minutes to break apart. Scoop slush into tall serving glasses. Drizzle with orange-flavored liqueur. (If slush is too hard to scoop, let stand at room temperature for 5 to 10 minutes to soften.)

Per Serving: Calories: 148 • Protein: 0 • Carbohydrate: 38 g.
• Fat: 0 • Cholesterol: 0 • Sodium: 8 mg.
Exchanges: 2½ fruit

Strawberry-Banana Slush

  1½ cups hot water
   1 cup sugar
   3 ripe medium bananas, mashed
   2 cups whole strawberries, hulled
  ½ cup orange juice
   2 tablespoons lemon juice

5 servings

In 4-cup measure, combine water and sugar. Stir until sugar is dissolved. Set aside.

In food processor or blender, combine bananas, strawberries and juices. Process until smooth. Stir in sugar mixture.

Pour mixture into 11 x 7-inch baking dish. Freeze at least 3 hours, or until firm, stirring every hour to break apart. Scoop slush into tall serving glasses. Add chilled carbonated water, lemon-lime soda or ginger ale, if desired. (If slush is too hard to scoop, let stand at room temperature for 5 to 10 minutes to soften.)

Per Serving: Calories: 248 • Protein: 1 g. • Carbohydrate: 63 g.
• Fat: 1 g. • Cholesterol: 0 • Sodium: 3 mg.
Exchanges: 4 fruit

Rhubarb Slush

3 cups chopped rhubarb
3 cups hot water
1 cup raisins
1 tablespoon grated orange peel
1/3 cup sugar
2 cups chilled carbonated water or
    lemon-lime soda

4 servings

In 3-quart casserole, combine rhubarb, water, raisins and peel. Cover. Microwave at High for 14 to 16 minutes, or until rhubarb softens, stirring twice. Let stand, covered, for 10 minutes. Strain mixture through fine-mesh strainer into large mixing bowl, pressing with back of spoon to release juice. Discard pulp. Add sugar. Stir until sugar is dissolved. Pour juice into ice cube trays and freeze at least 3 hours.

Remove cubes from trays. Place cubes and carbonated water in food processor or blender. Process until smooth. Pour into tall serving glasses. Garnish with additional grated peel, if desired.

Variation: Prepare as directed above, except place 3 or 4 cubes in each serving glass. Pour chilled carbonated water, lemon-lime soda or ginger ale over cubes.

Per Serving: Calories: 198 • Protein: 2 g. • Carbohydrate: 51 g.
• Fat: 0 • Cholesterol: 0 • Sodium: 9 mg.
Exchanges: 3¼ fruit

Melon Slush

6 cups cubed watermelon (1-inch cubes),
    seeds removed
1 can (6 oz.) frozen orange juice
    concentrate, defrosted
1/2 cup honeydew melon balls (3/4-inch)
1/2 cup cantaloupe melon balls (3/4-inch)
1/2 cup halved seedless red grapes

6 servings

In food processor or blender, process watermelon until smooth. Add concentrate. Process until smooth. Add remaining ingredients. Stir to combine.

Pour mixture into 11 x 7-inch baking dish. Freeze at least 3 hours, or until firm, stirring every 30 minutes to break apart. Scoop slush into tall serving glasses. (If slush is too hard to scoop, let stand at room temperature for 5 to 10 minutes to soften.)

Per Serving: Calories: 122 • Protein: 2 g. • Carbohydrate: 29 g.
• Fat: 1 g. • Cholesterol: 0 • Sodium: 7 mg.
Exchanges: 2 fruit

◄ Tri-Tropical Fruit Spritzers

½ cup grapefruit juice
1 ripe medium banana, mashed
½ cup finely chopped peeled kiwifruit
½ cup sugar
1 tablespoon lemon juice
1 tablespoon orange juice
6 cups chilled carbonated water, lemon-lime
    soda or sparkling white wine

6 servings

In 1½-quart casserole, combine all ingredients, except carbonated water. Cover. Microwave at High for 3 to 4 minutes, or until sugar is dissolved, stirring once. Spoon mixture into food processor or blender. Process until smooth.

Pack tall serving glasses with crushed ice. Place ¼ cup fruit syrup and 1 cup carbonated water in each glass. Mix well.

Variation 1: Prepare recipe as directed above, except substitute chopped mango, chopped papaya and chopped pineapple for grapefruit juice, banana and kiwifruit. Microwave at High for 4 to 6 minutes.

Variation 2: Prepare recipe as directed above, except substitute 1 scoop vanilla ice cream for crushed ice.

Per Serving: Calories: 100 • Protein: 0 • Carbohydrate: 25 g.
• Fat: 0 • Cholesterol: 0 • Sodium: 1 mg.
Exchanges: 1¾ fruit

Wassail

1 medium seedless orange
24 whole cloves
2 cups red wine
2 cups apple cider
¼ cup sugar
2 teaspoons grated lemon peel
2 slices peeled fresh gingerroot
1 small stick cinnamon
¼ teaspoon ground nutmeg
¼ teaspoon ground allspice

8 servings

Cut orange into 8 wedges. Insert 3 cloves into rind of each wedge. Set aside. In 8-cup measure, combine remaining ingredients. Stir until sugar is dissolved. Add orange wedges. Cover with plastic wrap. Microwave at High for 11 to 15 minutes, or just until boiling. Let stand, covered, for 10 minutes. Remove plastic wrap. Discard cinnamon stick. Serve hot.

Per Serving: Calories: 106 • Protein: 0 • Carbohydrate: 18 g.
• Fat: 0 • Cholesterol: 0 • Sodium: 6 mg.
Exchanges: 1¾ fruit

Rhubarb-Mint Juice ▶

1 lb. rhubarb, chopped
  (3 cups)
3 cups hot water
1/2 cup snipped fresh mint
  leaves
1/2 cup sugar

4 servings

In 3-quart casserole, combine rhubarb, water and mint leaves. Cover. Microwave at High for 10 to 14 minutes, or until rhubarb softens, stirring twice.

Strain mixture through fine-mesh strainer into large mixing bowl, pressing with back of spoon to release juice. Discard pulp. Add sugar. Stir until sugar is dissolved. Serve warm, or chill and serve over ice.

Per Serving: Calories: 115 • Protein: 1 g.
• Carbohydrate: 29 g. • Fat: 0
• Cholesterol: 0 • Sodium: 4 mg.
Exchanges: 2 fruit

Iced Orange Café au Lait

4 cups hot water
2 tablespoons instant coffee
  crystals
1 tablespoon grated orange
  peel
4 cups cold milk

8 servings

Place water in 8-cup measure. Cover with plastic wrap. Microwave at High for 6 to 11 minutes, or until boiling. Add coffee crystals and peel. Stir until crystals are dissolved. Re-cover. Cool to room temperature.

Pack tall serving glasses with crushed ice. Pour 1/2 cup coffee and 1/2 cup milk simultaneously over ice. Top with additional grated peel, if desired.

Per Serving: Calories: 77 • Protein: 4 g.
• Carbohydrate: 6 g. • Fat: 4 g.
• Cholesterol: 17 mg. • Sodium: 60 mg.
Exchanges: 1/2 low-fat milk, 3/4 fat

Raspberry-Chocolate Coffee

2 cups red raspberries
2/3 cup sugar
2 tablespoons orange juice
3/4 cup chocolate syrup
9 cups hot coffee

12 servings

In 1 1/2-quart casserole, combine raspberries, sugar and juice. Cover. Microwave at High for 3 to 4 minutes, or until sugar is dissolved, stirring once. Spoon mixture into food processor or blender. Process until smooth.

Strain mixture through fine-mesh strainer into 4-cup measure, pressing with back of spoon to release juice. Discard pulp and seeds. In each coffee cup, combine 1 tablespoon raspberry syrup and 1 tablespoon chocolate syrup. Add 3/4 cup coffee. Mix well.

Per Serving: Calories: 99 • Protein: 1 g. • Carbohydrate: 26 g. • Fat: 0
• Cholesterol: 0 • Sodium: 22 mg.
Exchanges: 1 3/4 fruit

◄ Vegetable-Herb Bouillon

4   cups hot water
1   cup finely chopped onions
1   medium tomato, chopped (1 cup)
1   cup finely chopped leek
½   cup finely chopped carrot
½   cup finely chopped celery
¼   to ½ cup finely chopped turnip
¼   cup snipped fresh parsley
2   tablespoons snipped fresh basil leaves
1   tablespoon fresh thyme leaves
2   cloves garlic
2   teaspoons lemon juice
1   teaspoon salt
½   teaspoon freshly ground pepper

6 to 8 servings

Place water in 3-quart casserole. Cover. Micro-wave at High for 9 to 15 minutes, or until boiling. Stir in remaining ingredients. Re-cover. Micro-wave at 50% (Medium) for 30 to 40 minutes, or until vegetables are tender, stirring every 10 min-utes. Let stand, covered, for 20 minutes.

Strain mixture through cheesecloth-lined strainer into large mixing bowl, pressing with back of spoon to remove excess moisture. Discard vegetables. Serve bouillon hot or chilled. Sprinkle with snipped fresh chives, if desired.

Per Serving: Calories: 23 • Protein: 1 g. • Carbohydrate: 5 g.
• Fat: 0 • Cholesterol: 0 • Sodium: 290 mg.
Exchanges: 1 vegetable

Fresh Carrot Juice

2½   cups water, divided
2   cups thinly sliced carrots
1   teaspoon instant chicken bouillon granules

6 servings

In 2-quart casserole, combine ½ cup water, the carrots and bouillon. Cover. Microwave at High for 12 to 14 minutes, or until carrots are tender, stirring once or twice. Spoon mixture into food processor or blender. Process until smooth. Add remaining 2 cups water. Process until smooth. Chill 1 to 2 hours, or until cold.

Per Serving: Calories: 17 • Protein: 0 • Carbohydrate: 4 g.
• Fat: 0 • Cholesterol: 0 • Sodium: 173 mg.
Exchanges: ¾ vegetable

Fresh Tomato Juice

4   medium tomatoes
1½   teaspoons sugar
½   teaspoon salt

5 to 6 servings

Cut each tomato into 10 wedges. Place in 2-quart casserole. Cover. Microwave at High for 6 to 9 minutes, or until tomatoes are hot, stirring twice.

Strain tomatoes through fine-mesh strainer into 4-cup measure, pressing with back of spoon to release juice. Discard pulp and seeds. Stir in sugar and salt. Chill 1 to 2 hours, or until cold.

Per Serving: Calories: 37 • Protein: 1 g. • Carbohydrate: 8 g.
• Fat: 1 g. • Cholesterol: 0 • Sodium: 196 mg.
Exchanges: 1½ vegetable

Virgin Mary ▶

2½ cups Fresh Tomato Juice, opposite
¼ cup lime juice
1 tablespoon Worcestershire sauce
1 teaspoon horseradish sauce
¾ teaspoon hot pepper sauce
½ teaspoon ground cumin
¼ teaspoon celery salt
¼ teaspoon freshly ground pepper
6 asparagus spears, trimmed (optional)

6 servings

In 4-cup measure, combine all ingredients, except asparagus. Add asparagus spears to juice
mixture. Refrigerate overnight. Pack tall serving
glasses with crushed ice. Pour mixture over ice.
Add 1 asparagus spear to each glass.

Variation: To make Bloody Mary, prepare as directed above, except add 3 oz. vodka to each glass.

Per Serving: Calories: 36 • Protein: 1 g. • Carbohydrate: 8 g.
• Fat: 0 • Cholesterol: 0 • Sodium: 269 mg.
Exchanges: 1½ vegetable

Vegetable Revitalizer ▶

½ cup finely chopped seeded peeled
    cucumber
½ cup finely chopped celery
½ cup torn spinach leaves
⅓ cup finely chopped carrot
¼ cup finely chopped peeled beet*
¼ cup snipped watercress leaves
2 tablespoons finely chopped onion
1 tablespoon soy sauce
1 tablespoon Worcestershire sauce
1 teaspoon instant chicken bouillon granules
    dissolved in ¼ cup hot water
½ teaspoon freshly ground pepper
2½ cups Fresh Tomato Juice, opposite

8 servings

In food processor or blender, combine all ingredients, except tomato juice. Process until smooth.
Blend in juice. Chill 1 to 2 hours, or until cold.
Serve with cucumber spear or dollop of plain
yogurt, if desired.

*Wear gloves when working with beet to avoid
staining hands.

Per Serving: Calories: 35 • Protein: 1 g. • Carbohydrate: 8 g.
• Fat: 0 • Cholesterol: 0 • Sodium: 407 mg.
Exchanges: 1½ vegetable

Fresh Starts

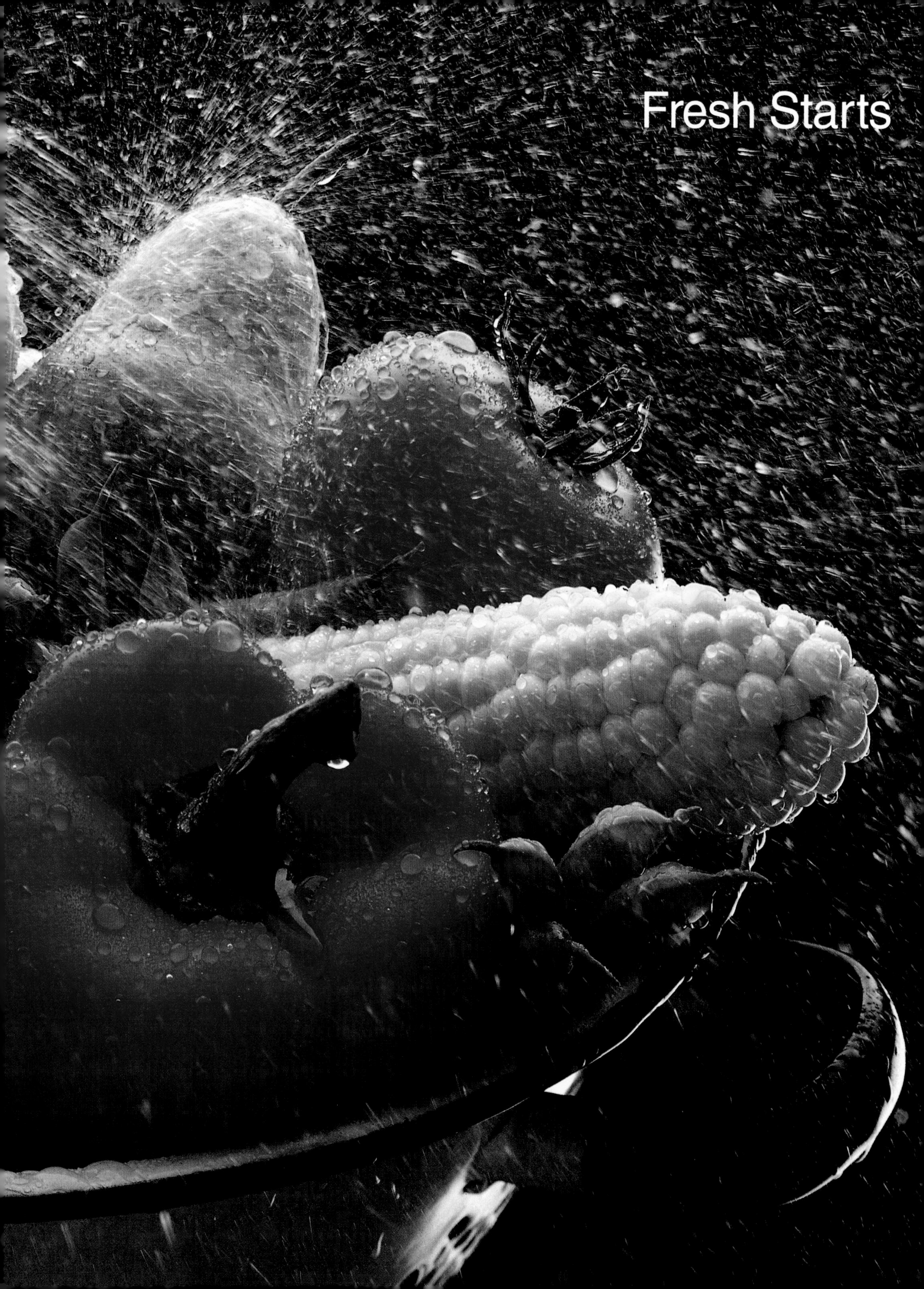

Marinara Sauce ▼

½ cup chopped Vidalia onion
1 tablespoon olive oil
7 Roma tomatoes, chopped (3½ cups)
¼ cup tomato paste
1 tablespoon snipped fresh oregano leaves
1 teaspoon fresh thyme leaves
½ teaspoon sugar

8 servings

In 2-quart casserole, combine onion and oil. Cover. Microwave at High for 3½ to 4 minutes, or until onion is tender, stirring once. Add remaining ingredients. Mix well. Microwave at High, uncovered, for 13 to 15 minutes, or until mixture thickens and flavors are blended, stirring 2 or 3 times. Serve as sauce with Potato Cheese Sticks, below.

Per Serving: Calories: 45 • Protein: 1 g. • Carbohydrate: 7 g.
• Fat: 2 g. • Cholesterol: 0 • Sodium: 73 mg.
Exchanges: 1 vegetable, ½ fat

Potato Cheese Sticks ▼

4 medium russet potatoes, peeled and cut into 1-inch cubes (4 cups)
½ cup water
¼ cup shredded fresh Parmesan cheese
¼ teaspoon garlic powder
¼ teaspoon seasoned salt
⅛ teaspoon pepper
⅛ teaspoon cayenne
4 oz. mozzarella cheese, cut into 3 × ¼ × ¼-inch strips
½ cup seasoned dry bread crumbs
Vegetable oil

8 servings

In 2-quart casserole, combine potatoes and water. Cover. Microwave at High for 12 to 19 minutes, or until potatoes are very tender, stirring once or twice. Let stand, covered, for 5 minutes. Drain.

Add Parmesan cheese, garlic powder, seasoned salt, pepper and cayenne. Mash with potato masher until mixture is smooth. Shape about 3 tablespoons potato mixture around each strip of cheese, enclosing cheese. Roll potato sticks in bread crumbs.

In 10-inch nonstick skillet, heat ⅛ inch oil conventionally over medium-high heat. Cook potato cheese sticks, 4 at a time, for 3 to 5 minutes, or until golden brown on all sides. Drain on paper-towel-lined plate. Serve with Marinara Sauce, above.

Per Serving: Calories: 208 • Protein: 7 g. • Carbohydrate: 21 g.
• Fat: 11 g. • Cholesterol: 14 mg. • Sodium: 340 mg.
Exchanges: 1¼ starch, ½ high-fat meat, 1¼ fat

Asparagus Guacamole ▲

1 lb. asparagus spears, cut into 1-inch
   lengths (2 cups)
2 tablespoons water
1 medium tomato, seeded and chopped
   (1 cup)
2 tablespoons sour cream
2 tablespoons sliced green onion
1 tablespoon olive oil
1 tablespoon lemon juice
1 teaspoon ground cumin
1 clove garlic, minced
1/2 teaspoon dried oregano leaves
1/4 teaspoon salt
1/4 teaspoon cayenne

12 servings

In 2-quart casserole, combine asparagus and water. Cover. Microwave at High for 6 to 8 minutes, or until asparagus is tender, stirring once. Rinse with cold water. Drain.

In food processor or blender, process asparagus until smooth. Place in medium mixing bowl. Add remaining ingredients. Mix well. Serve with tortilla chips, if desired.

Per Serving: Calories: 27 • Protein: 1 g. • Carbohydrate: 2 g.
• Fat: 2 g. • Cholesterol: 1 mg. • Sodium: 49 mg.
Exchanges: 1/2 vegetable, 1/2 fat

Lone Star Caviar ▲

1 pkg. (10 oz.) frozen black-eyed peas
1/2 cup water
2 medium tomatoes, seeded and chopped
   (2 cups)
1 medium green pepper, chopped (1 1/3 cups)
1/2 cup sliced green onions
1/2 cup snipped fresh cilantro leaves
1/4 cup lemon juice
1/4 cup olive oil
2 serrano peppers, seeded and finely
   chopped
1 to 2 jalapeño peppers, seeded and finely
   chopped
2 cloves garlic, minced
1/2 teaspoon salt
1/4 teaspoon ground cumin

16 servings

In 2-quart casserole, combine peas and water. Cover. Microwave at High for 12 to 14 minutes, or until peas are tender, stirring once. Let stand, covered, for 5 minutes. Rinse with cold water. Drain. In medium mixing bowl, combine peas and remaining ingredients. Cover with plastic wrap. Chill at least 4 hours. Serve with tortilla chips, if desired.

Per Serving: Calories: 64 • Protein: 2 g. • Carbohydrate: 7 g.
• Fat: 4 g. • Cholesterol: 0 • Sodium: 73 mg.
Exchanges: 1 vegetable, 3/4 fat

Natural Peanut Butter Fruit Dip ▲

Dip:

- 1 pkg. (8 oz.) cream cheese
- ¾ cup packed brown sugar
- ¼ cup granulated sugar
- ¼ cup 100% natural creamy peanut butter
- ¼ cup chopped dry-roasted peanuts

- 4 cups water
- ¼ cup lemon juice
- 2 medium green eating apples, cored and sliced
- 1 medium red eating apple, cored and sliced
- 2 cups whole strawberries, hulled
  Celery sticks, tops included

14 servings

In small mixing bowl, microwave cream cheese at 50% (Medium) for 1½ to 3 minutes, or until softened. Add remaining dip ingredients. Mix well. Set aside.

In large mixing bowl, combine water and juice. Immerse apple slices in water mixture to prevent discoloring. Drain. Arrange dip, apple slices, strawberries and celery sticks on serving platter. Garnish dip with additional chopped peanuts, if desired.

Per Serving: Calories: 191 • Protein: 3 g. • Carbohydrate: 25 g.
• Fat: 9 g. • Cholesterol: 18 mg. • Sodium: 70 mg.
Exchanges: ½ high-fat meat, 1¾ fruit, 1 fat

Steamed Vegetable Platter with Minted Aioli

- 2 cups hot water
- ¼ cup loosely packed fresh mint leaves
- 3 cloves garlic, minced
- ¼ teaspoon olive oil
- ⅔ cup mayonnaise
- 1 tablespoon lemon juice
- 1½ cups snow pea pods
- 4 small red potatoes, quartered
- 4 oz. Brussels sprouts, trimmed and cut in half
- 1 medium red pepper, cut into ½-inch wedges
- 1 tablespoon water
- 8 green onions, trimmed to 6-inch lengths

4 servings

Place water in 4-cup measure. Cover with plastic wrap. Microwave at High for 4 to 6 minutes, or until boiling. Remove plastic wrap. Immerse mint leaves in hot water for 3 seconds, or just until wilted. Remove with slotted spoon. Rinse with cold water. Drain, pressing with back of spoon to remove excess moisture. Finely snip leaves. Set aside.

In small bowl, combine garlic and oil. Microwave at High for 1 to 1½ minutes, or until tender. With back of spoon, mash garlic mixture into a paste. In small mixing bowl, combine mint, garlic mixture, mayonnaise and juice. Whisk until blended. Set aioli aside.

Arrange pea pods in center of 10-inch round plate. Arrange potatoes, Brussels sprouts and pepper wedges around pea pods, leaving space for onions. Sprinkle with water. Cover with plastic wrap. Microwave at High for 6 to 8 minutes, or until potatoes are tender-crisp, rotating plate once or twice. Pierce plastic wrap with tip of knife to release steam. Let stand, covered, for 5 minutes. Remove plastic wrap. Arrange onions on plate. Serve with aioli.

Per Serving: Calories: 353 • Protein: 4 g. • Carbohydrate: 20 g.
• Fat: 30 g. • Cholesterol: 22 mg. • Sodium: 227 mg.
Exchanges: ½ starch, 2½ vegetable, 6 fat

Steamed Vegetable Platter with Curried Hummus Dip

Dip:

- 1 can (19 oz.) garbanzo beans (chick-peas), rinsed and drained
- 2 tablespoons olive oil
- 2 tablespoons snipped fresh parsley
- 1 to 2 tablespoons lemon juice
- 1 tablespoon sesame oil
- 2 teaspoons soy sauce
- 1 clove garlic, minced
- ¼ teaspoon freshly ground pepper
- ¼ teaspoon curry powder

- 1 medium artichoke (12 oz.)
- 1 tablespoon lemon juice
- 5 oz. baby zucchini (about 12)
- 2 cups cauliflowerets
- 5 oz. baby carrots (1 cup)
- 2 tablespoons water

4 to 6 servings

In food processor, combine all dip ingredients. Process until smooth, scraping sides of bowl periodically. Set hummus aside.

Trim artichoke 1 inch from top and close to base. Cut off sharp tips of outer leaves. Rinse; shake off excess water. Brush with 1 tablespoon juice. Wrap in plastic wrap. Microwave at High for 5 minutes. Remove plastic wrap and place artichoke at one end of 12 × 10-inch serving platter.

Starting ¾ inch from end of each zucchini, cut ¼-inch strips, leaving strips attached to stem end. Arrange zucchini in center of platter, pressing lightly to fan. Arrange cauliflower and carrots alternately around edge of platter. Sprinkle with water. Cover platter with plastic wrap.

Microwave at High for 6 to 8 minutes, or until vegetables are tender-crisp, fork can be easily inserted in base of artichoke and leaves can be removed with slight tug, rotating platter once or twice. Pierce plastic wrap with tip of knife to release steam. Let stand, covered, for 5 minutes. Remove plastic wrap. Re-fan zucchini. Serve with hummus.

Per Serving: Calories: 157 • Protein: 5 g. • Carbohydrate: 17 g.
• Fat: 8 g. • Cholesterol: 0 • Sodium: 251 mg.
Exchanges: ½ starch, 2 vegetable, 1½ fat

Steamed Vegetable Platter with Raclette

3 small red potatoes, cut into
 ¼-inch slices, rinsed
2 tablespoons water, divided
4 oz. Monterey Jack cheese,
 cut into 1-inch cubes
5 oz. red pearl onions (1 cup)
1 cup broccoli flowerets
4 oz. whole mushrooms,
 stems removed (1 cup)
1 tablespoon snipped fresh
 chives

4 servings

In 1-quart casserole, combine potato slices and 1 tablespoon water. Cover. Microwave at High for 5 to 6 minutes, or until tender-crisp, stirring once. Drain.

Place cheese in small bowl. Place bowl in center of 10-inch round plate. Arrange potato slices, onions, broccoli and mushrooms around bowl. Sprinkle vegetables with remaining 1 tablespoon water. Cover plate with plastic wrap.

Microwave at High for 6 to 7 minutes, or until vegetables are tender-crisp and cheese is melted and bubbly, rotating plate once or twice. Stir chives into cheese. Serve cheese with vegetables.

Per Serving: Calories: 170 • Protein: 10 g. • Carbohydrate: 14 g. • Fat: 9 g.
• Cholesterol: 25 mg. • Sodium: 167 mg.
Exchanges: ½ starch, 1 high-fat meat, 1¼ vegetable

Vegetable Nachos ▼

¼ cup plus 2 tablespoons
 refried beans
½ teaspoon ground cumin
1 medium zucchini, cut into
 ¼-inch slices (1 cup)
2 jalapeño or chili peppers,
 thinly sliced
6 cherry tomatoes, thinly
 sliced
¼ cup shredded Cheddar
 cheese

6 servings

In small mixing bowl, combine refried beans and cumin. Spread about 1 teaspoon bean mixture on top of each zucchini slice. Arrange slices on serving plate. Top evenly with pepper and tomato slices and cheese. Microwave at High for 3 to 4 minutes, or until nachos are hot and cheese just begins to melt.

Variation: Prepare recipe as directed above, except substitute 4 to 5 small red potatoes for zucchini. Peel potatoes and place in 1-quart casserole with 2 tablespoons water. Cover. Microwave at High for 3 to 5 minutes, or until potatoes are tender-crisp. Let stand, covered, for 5 minutes. Drain. Cool slightly. Cut each potato into ¼-inch slices. Arrange slices on serving plate. Continue with recipe as directed above.

Per Serving: Calories: 45 • Protein: 3 g.
• Carbohydrate: 5 g. • Fat: 2 g.
• Cholesterol: 5 mg. • Sodium: 99 mg.
Exchanges: 1 vegetable, ½ fat

Eggplant Spread with Balsamic Vinegar

- 1 medium eggplant (1 lb.), peeled and cut into 1/2-inch cubes
- 1/2 teaspoon salt
- 1/4 cup thinly sliced green onions
- 2 tablespoons snipped drained roasted red peppers
- 2 tablespoons balsamic vinegar
- 1 tablespoon fresh thyme leaves
- 1 tablespoon olive oil
- 1 clove garlic, minced
- 1/4 teaspoon freshly ground pepper

6 servings

In medium mixing bowl, combine eggplant and salt. Toss to coat. Let stand for 30 minutes, stirring once or twice. Blot eggplant with paper towels to remove excess moisture. Add remaining ingredients. Mix well. Spread mixture in 10-inch square casserole. Microwave at High for 12 to 15 minutes, or until eggplant is tender, stirring twice. Chill. Serve on slices of crusty French bread.

Per Serving: Calories: 40 • Protein: 1 g.
• Carbohydrate: 5 g. • Fat: 2 g.
• Cholesterol: 0 • Sodium: 93 mg.
Exchanges: 1 vegetable, 1/2 fat

Caponata ▲

- 1/4 cup plus 1 tablespoon olive oil, divided
- 1 medium eggplant (1 lb.), cut into 3/4-inch cubes
- 1 clove garlic, minced
- 1 teaspoon salt
- 1/2 cup chopped onion
- 1/3 cup sliced celery
- 1 can (16 oz.) Roma tomatoes, drained and cut up
- 1/3 cup halved pitted medium black olives
- 1/4 cup red wine vinegar
- 1 tablespoon capers, drained
- 1 tablespoon snipped fresh oregano leaves
- 1/4 teaspoon freshly ground pepper
- 1/4 cup toasted pine nuts
  Toasted Italian or French bread slices
  Margarine or butter
  Shredded fresh Parmesan cheese

16 servings

In 12-inch nonstick skillet, heat 1/4 cup oil conventionally over medium heat. Add eggplant, garlic and salt. Cook for 5 to 7 minutes, or until eggplant is golden brown, stirring occasionally. Remove from heat. Set aside.

In 2-quart casserole, combine remaining 1 tablespoon oil, the onion and celery. Microwave at High for 5 to 7 minutes, or until onion is tender, stirring once. Stir in tomatoes, olives, vinegar, capers, oregano and pepper. Cover. Microwave at High for 4 to 6 minutes, or until mixture is hot and flavors are blended, stirring once.

Stir in eggplant mixture and pine nuts. Cool slightly. Cover. Chill overnight, stirring occasionally. Serve on slices of toasted bread that have been buttered and sprinkled with Parmesan cheese.

Per Serving: Calories: 67 • Protein: 1 g. • Carbohydrate: 4 g. • Fat: 6 g.
• Cholesterol: 0 • Sodium: 225 mg.
Exchanges: 3/4 vegetable, 1 fat

Tangy Peach Chutney ▶ with Brie

4 medium peaches, peeled*
   and coarsely chopped
1/2 cup golden raisins
1/2 cup packed brown sugar
1/2 cup chopped red pepper
1/3 cup white vinegar
1 tablespoon grated lemon or
   orange peel
1 tablespoon grated fresh
   gingerroot
1 clove garlic, minced
1/4 teaspoon ground cinnamon
1/4 teaspoon ground allspice
1/4 teaspoon ground nutmeg
1 wheel (8 oz.) Brie cheese,
   4 1/2 x 1 1/2 inches
   Sliced almonds

6 servings

In 2-quart casserole, combine peaches and remaining ingredients, except Brie and almonds. Cover. Microwave at High for 10 minutes, stirring once. Uncover. Microwave at High for 20 to 25 minutes longer, or until chutney is thickened, stirring every 5 minutes.

Meanwhile, place Brie in center of serving plate. Microwave at 50% (Medium) for 45 seconds to 1 minute, or until slightly warm, rotating once. Spoon 1/2 cup warm chutney over Brie. Garnish with sliced almonds. Serve with crackers or slices of crusty French bread. Store remaining chutney in sealed container in refrigerator up to 1 month.

*See How to Peel Apricots, page 74.

Per Serving: Calories: 269 • Protein: 9 g.
• Carbohydrate: 37 g. • Fat: 11 g.
• Cholesterol: 38 mg. • Sodium: 245 mg.
Exchanges: 1 high-fat meat, 2 1/2 fruit,
1/2 fat

Sweet Hot Pepper Jelly* ▶

3 cups sugar
3 cups finely chopped red,
   green and yellow peppers
2 red chilies, thinly sliced
2 jalapeño peppers, thinly
   sliced
3/4 cup cider vinegar
1 pkg. (3 oz.) liquid fruit
   pectin

Three 1/2-pint jars

Sterilize jars and two-part sealing lids as directed by manufacturer. In 8-cup measure, combine all ingredients, except pectin. Microwave at High for 10 to 13 minutes, or until mixture comes to full rolling boil, stirring once. Add pectin. Mix well. Microwave at High for 20 to 25 minutes, or until jelly thickens and coats metal spoon, stirring frequently and watching closely to prevent boil-over.

Remove from microwave with hot pads. Ladle into prepared jars to within 1/8 inch of tops. Wipe jar rims and threads. Cover quickly with lids. Invert jars for 5 minutes; turn upright. After 1 hour, check lid seals. If not sealed, use jelly immediately. During cooling, invert jars once for several minutes to keep peppers evenly dispersed in jelly. Serve jelly on crackers with cream cheese or use as condiment with meats.

*Recipe not recommended for ovens with less than 600 cooking watts.

Per Serving: Calories: 51 • Protein: 0 • Carbohydrate: 13 g. • Fat: 0
• Cholesterol: 0 • Sodium: 0
Exchanges: 1 fruit

Basil & Walnut Pesto Canapés ▶

2 cups hot water
2 cups packed fresh basil
   leaves
4 oz. cream cheese
1/2 cup chopped walnuts or
   pecans, divided
1 clove garlic, minced
1/4 teaspoon grated lemon peel
1 medium zucchini, thinly
   sliced (1 cup)

8 to 10 servings

Place water in 4-cup measure. Cover with plastic wrap. Microwave at High for 4 to 6 minutes, or until boiling. Remove plastic wrap. Immerse basil leaves in hot water for 3 seconds, or just until wilted. Remove with slotted spoon. Rinse with cold water. Drain, pressing with back of spoon to remove excess moisture. Set aside.

In small mixing bowl, microwave cream cheese at High for 30 to 45 seconds, or until softened. Add basil, 1/4 cup walnuts, the garlic and lemon peel. Mix well.

Sprinkle remaining 1/4 cup walnuts on sheet of plastic wrap. Spoon cheese mixture onto plastic wrap. Use plastic wrap to shape mixture into log, 1 1/2 inches in diameter, pressing so that nuts adhere to log. Chill 1 to 2 hours, or until firm. Cut into 1/2-inch slices. Top each zucchini slice with cheese log slice.

Per Serving: Calories: 91 • Protein: 2 g. • Carbohydrate: 5 g. • Fat: 8 g.
• Cholesterol: 12 mg. • Sodium: 36 mg.
Exchanges: 1/4 high-fat meat, 1 vegetable, 1 fat

Garden-stuffed Mini Cream Puffs

 1   cup hot water
 ½   cup margarine or butter
 1¼ cups all-purpose flour
 ¼   teaspoon salt
 4   eggs

Filling:

 1   pkg. (8 oz.) cream cheese
 8   cups chopped spinach
     leaves
 ¼   cup chopped red pepper
 ¼   cup grated carrot
 1   tablespoon snipped fresh
     dill weed
 ¼   teaspoon salt

8 servings

Per Serving: Calories: 326 • Protein: 9 g.
• Carbohydrate: 19 g. • Fat: 24 g.
• Cholesterol: 137 mg. • Sodium: 430 mg.
Exchanges: 1 starch, ½ medium-fat meat,
½ vegetable, 4½ fat

How to Make Garden-stuffed Mini Cream Puffs

Heat conventional oven to 400°F. Spray 2 large baking sheets with nonstick vegetable cooking spray. Set aside. In 8-cup measure, combine water and margarine.

Microwave at High for 3 to 5 minutes, or until margarine is melted. Add flour and salt. Stir vigorously until mixture forms ball. Add 1 egg at a time, beating after each addition.

Remove from baking sheets. Cut each cream puff in half crosswise. Set aside. Place cream cheese in small mixing bowl. Microwave at 50% (Medium) for 1½ to 3 minutes, or until softened. Set aside.

Place spinach in 2-quart casserole. Cover. Microwave at High for 2 to 3 minutes, or just until wilted. Drain, pressing with back of spoon to remove excess moisture.

Drop dough by heaping table-spoons onto prepared baking sheets, spacing at least 1 inch apart. Bake for 23 to 25 minutes, or until puffed and golden. Cool for 20 minutes.

Add spinach and remaining filling ingredients to cream cheese. Mix well. Spoon scant 1 tablespoon mixture into each cream puff. Serve immediately.

Stuffed Baby Potatoes

10 small red potatoes	2 tablespoons snipped fresh
3 tablespoons olive oil,	oregano leaves
divided	1 clove garlic, minced
1/2 cup finely chopped red	1/4 teaspoon freshly ground
onion	pepper
1/2 cup finely chopped green	1/4 cup shredded fresh
pepper	Parmesan cheese, divided
2 tablespoons snipped	
drained oil-pack sun-dried	
tomatoes	

8 to 10 servings

Pierce each potato with fork. Arrange in single layer on paper towel in microwave. Microwave at High for 12 to 15 minutes, or until tender, turning over and rearranging twice. Cool slightly. Heat conventional oven to 475°F. Slice each potato in half. Scoop out pulp, leaving 1/8-inch-thick shell. Reserve pulp. Brush shells evenly with 1 table-spoon oil. Arrange cut-sides-down on large baking sheet. Bake for 15 to 18 minutes, or until crispy and golden brown.

Meanwhile, in 1 1/2-quart casserole, combine remaining 2 tablespoons oil, the onion and green pepper. Microwave at High for 4 to 6 minutes, or until vegetables are tender, stirring once. Stir in tomatoes, oregano, garlic and pepper. Microwave at High for 1 to 2 minutes, or until mixture is hot and flavors are blended. Add reserved potato pulp. Mix well, stirring to coarsely mash potatoes.

Sprinkle insides of potato shells evenly with 2 tablespoons Parmesan cheese. Spoon heaping tablespoon potato mixture into each shell. Sprinkle tops evenly with remaining 2 tablespoons Parmesan cheese. Reduce oven temperature to 425°F. Bake stuffed shells for 15 to 18 minutes, or until golden brown. Serve with sour cream and snipped fresh chives, if desired.

Per Serving: Calories: 117 • Protein: 3 g. • Carbohydrate: 14 g. • Fat: 6 g.
• Cholesterol: 2 mg. • Sodium: 116 mg.
Exchanges: 1/2 starch, 1 1/2 vegetable, 1 fat

Savory Stuffed Artichokes

2 medium artichokes
  (12 oz. each)
2 tablespoons lemon juice
¼ cup water
⅓ cup finely chopped shallots
¼ cup finely chopped red
  pepper
1 tablespoon olive oil
1 clove garlic, minced
1 cup seasoned dry bread
  crumbs
¼ cup dry white wine
¼ teaspoon freshly ground
  pepper
2 tablespoons shredded
  fresh Parmesan cheese

2 to 4 servings

Trim artichokes 1 inch from top and close to base. Cut off sharp tips of outer leaves. Rinse; shake off excess water. Brush with juice. In 8-inch square baking dish, combine artichokes and water. Cover with plastic wrap. Microwave at High for 6 to 8 minutes, or just until hot, rotating dish once. Remove plastic wrap. Set dish aside.

In 1-quart casserole, combine shallots, red pepper, oil and garlic. Microwave at High for 4 to 5 minutes, or until shallots are tender. Stir in crumbs, wine and pepper. Spoon crumb mixture between leaves of artichokes.

Return artichokes to baking dish. Cover with plastic wrap. Microwave at High for 7 to 9 minutes, or until fork can be easily inserted in base of artichokes and leaves can be removed with slight tug, rotating dish once. Pierce plastic wrap with tip of knife to release steam. Let stand, covered, for 10 minutes. Transfer artichokes to serving platter. Before serving, sprinkle evenly with Parmesan cheese.

Per Serving: Calories: 206 • Protein: 8 g.
• Carbohydrate: 31 g. • Fat: 5 g.
• Cholesterol 4 mg. • Sodium: 873 mg.
Exchanges: 1½ starch, 1½ vegetable,
1 fat

Tabbouleh-stuffed Avocados ▲

½ cup water
¼ cup uncooked bulgur
  (cracked wheat)
1 small tomato, seeded and
  finely chopped (½ cup)
½ cup snipped fresh parsley
¼ cup thinly sliced green
  onions

Dressing:
1 to 2 tablespoons lemon
  juice
1 tablespoon olive oil
¼ teaspoon salt

2 ripe avocados, cut in half
  lengthwise

4 servings

Place water in 2-cup measure. Microwave at High for 1¾ to 2½ minutes, or until boiling. Stir in bulgur. Let stand for 30 minutes. Drain, pressing with back of spoon to remove excess moisture.

In medium mixing bowl, combine bulgur, tomato, parsley and onions. In small bowl, combine dressing ingredients. Add dressing to tabbouleh salad. Toss to coat. Spoon salad evenly into avocado halves. Serve immediately.

Per Serving: Calories: 232 • Protein: 4 g. • Carbohydrate: 16 g. • Fat: 19 g.
• Cholesterol: 0 • Sodium: 154 mg.
Exchanges: ½ starch, 1½ vegetable, 4 fat

Stuffed Vegetable Platter

4 oz. cream cheese
1 tablespoon snipped drained oil-pack sun-dried tomatoes
1 tablespoon shredded fresh Parmesan cheese
1 tablespoon snipped fresh chives

Vegetables:
Hollowed-out cherry tomatoes
Whole mushrooms, stems removed
Celery stalks, cut into 2-inch lengths
Snow pea pods, opened
Steamed baby carrots*

4 servings

In small mixing bowl, microwave cream cheese at High for 30 to 45 seconds, or until softened, stirring once. Stir in sun-dried tomatoes, Parmesan cheese and chives. Spoon or pipe cheese mixture into one or more of desired vegetables. Garnish with additional snipped fresh chives, if desired.

* In 1-quart casserole, combine 2½ oz. baby carrots (½ cup) and 2 teaspoons water. Cover. Microwave at High for 1½ to 2 minutes, or until carrots are tender-crisp, stirring once. Drain. Cut lengthwise wedge into each carrot. Spoon or pipe cheese mixture into wedges. Trim with sprigs of fresh parsley to simulate carrot tops.

NOTE: Nutritional information given for cheese mixture only.

Per Serving: Calories: 118 • Protein: 3 g. • Carbohydrate: 1 g. • Fat: 11 g.
• Cholesterol: 32 mg. • Sodium: 193 mg.
Exchanges: ¼ high-fat meat, ¼ vegetable, 2 fat

Steamed Vegetable Platter with Herbed Hollandaise

8 oz. asparagus spears,
    trimmed to 6-inch lengths
1 medium yellow squash,
    diagonally sliced (1 cup)
1½ cups cauliflowerets
5 oz. baby carrots (1 cup)
¾ cup plus 2 tablespoons
    water, divided
1 pkg. (1¼ oz.) hollandaise
    sauce mix
1 tablespoon vegetable oil
2 teaspoons snipped fresh
    tarragon leaves

4 servings

Arrange asparagus spears in center of oval serving platter. Surround asparagus with squash slices. Encircle squash with cauliflower. Arrange carrots on edge of platter. Sprinkle with 2 tablespoons water. Cover with plastic wrap. Microwave at High for 8 to 10 minutes, or until vegetables are tender-crisp, rotating platter once or twice. Pierce plastic wrap with tip of knife to release steam. Let stand, covered, for 5 minutes.

Place sauce mix in medium mixing bowl. Blend in remaining ¾ cup water and the oil until smooth. Microwave at High for 4 to 5 minutes, or until sauce is thickened, stirring every minute. Stir in tarragon leaves. Serve hollandaise with vegetables.

Per Serving: Calories: 108 • Protein: 5 g. • Carbohydrate: 13 g. • Fat: 5 g.
• Cholesterol: 48 mg. • Sodium: 337 mg.
Exchanges: ¼ starch, 2 vegetable, 1 fat

Crispy Spiced Wontons

1 cup chopped shiitake
   mushrooms
1/4 cup thinly sliced green
   onions
2 teaspoons sesame oil
2 teaspoons oyster sauce
1 to 2 teaspoons grated fresh
   gingerroot
24 wonton skins (3 1/2-inch
   square)
   Water
   Vegetable oil

4 to 6 servings

Per Serving: Calories: 170 • Protein: 4 g.
• Carbohydrate: 15 g. • Fat: 11 g.
• Cholesterol: 0 • Sodium: 88 mg.
Exchanges: 2/3 starch, 1 vegetable, 2 fat

How to Make Crispy Spiced Wontons

Combine mushrooms, onions, sesame oil, oyster sauce and gingerroot in small mixing bowl.

Microwave at High for 3 to 4 minutes, or until mushrooms and onions are tender, stirring once. Place 1 teaspoon mushroom mixture on top corner of 1 wonton skin. Fold top corner over mixture and roll down halfway. Place dab of water on left corner.

Pull left and right corners back, placing right corner on top of water, and pinch together. Repeat with remaining mixture and wonton skins.

Heat 1/2 inch vegetable oil conventionally over medium heat in wok or wok skillet. Fry wontons, a few at a time, for 30 seconds to 1 minute, or until golden brown, turning occasionally. Drain on paper-towel-lined plate. Serve warm with sweet-and-sour sauce, hot mustard or soy sauce, if desired.

Spinach & Dill Turnovers with Yogurt Sauce

9 eggroll skins (7-inch square)

Filling:

4	cups shredded spinach leaves
1/3	cup sliced green onions
2	tablespoons snipped fresh dill weed
2	tablespoons olive oil
1/4	teaspoon cayenne
1/4	teaspoon garlic powder

Vegetable oil

Sauce:

1/2	cup finely chopped seeded cucumber
1/3	cup finely chopped seeded tomato
1/3	cup plain nonfat or low-fat yogurt
1/4	cup sour cream
1	tablespoon snipped fresh dill weed
1/2	teaspoon lemon juice

9 servings

Per Serving: Calories: 150 • Protein: 4 g. • Carbohydrate: 13 g.
• Fat: 9 g. • Cholesterol: 17 mg. • Sodium: 29 mg.
Exchanges: ¾ starch, ½ vegetable, 2 fat

How to Make Spinach & Dill Turnovers with Yogurt Sauce

Trim each eggroll skin to 6 x 6-inch square. (Reserve trimmings for Oriental Bow Ties, page 49, if desired.) Cover with plastic wrap. Set aside.

Combine filling ingredients in large mixing bowl. Place scant ½ cup filling in center of each eggroll skin. Brush edges lightly with water.

Fold bottom corner over filling to opposite corner, forming triangle. Press edges to seal. Place turnovers on plate. Cover with plastic wrap. Set aside.

Heat ¼ inch vegetable oil conventionally in 12-inch nonstick skillet over medium-high heat.

Add turnovers, 2 at a time, to skillet. Cook for 3 to 4 minutes, or until golden brown, turning over once.

Drain on paper-towel-lined plate. In small mixing bowl, combine sauce ingredients. Serve turnovers with sauce.

Potato & Chive Turnovers with Sweet Hot Carrot Salsa

Salsa:

- 1 cup finely chopped carrots
- 1/3 cup chopped green pepper
- 1 tablespoon olive oil
- 1/3 cup sliced green onions
- 2 tablespoons packed brown sugar
- 1 tablespoon white vinegar
- 1 tablespoon catsup
- 1 clove garlic, minced
- 1/4 teaspoon cayenne

- 9 eggroll skins (7-inch square)

Filling:

- 8 small red potatoes, peeled
- 1/2 cup water
- 1/2 cup shredded fresh Parmesan cheese
- 1/4 cup shredded carrot
- 1 tablespoon snipped fresh chives
- 1/4 teaspoon salt

  Vegetable oil

9 servings

In 1-quart casserole, combine carrots, green pepper and olive oil. Cover. Microwave at High for 2½ to 3½ minutes, or until carrots are tender, stirring once. Add remaining salsa ingredients. Mix well. Cover. Chill at least 2 hours, or until cold.

Trim each eggroll skin to 6 x 6-inch square. (Reserve trimmings for Oriental Bow Ties, page 49, if desired.) Cover with plastic wrap. Set aside. In 1-quart casserole, combine potatoes and water. Cover. Microwave at High for 9 to 11 minutes, or until potatoes are tender, stirring once. Drain. Cool completely. Shred potatoes. In medium mixing bowl, combine potatoes and remaining filling ingredients.

Place scant ½ cup filling in center of each eggroll skin. Brush edges lightly with water. Fold bottom corner over filling to opposite corner, forming triangle. Press edges to seal. Place turnovers on plate. Cover with plastic wrap. Set aside. In 12-inch nonstick skillet, heat ¼ inch vegetable oil conventionally over medium-high heat. Add turnovers, 2 at a time, to skillet. Cook for 3 to 4 minutes, or until golden brown, turning over once. Drain on paper-towel-lined plate. Serve turnovers with salsa.

Per Serving: Calories: 194 • Protein: 6 g. • Carbohydrate: 25 g. • Fat: 8 g.
• Cholesterol: 19 mg. • Sodium: 196 mg.
Exchanges: 1¼ starch, ¼ high-fat meat, 1¼ vegetable, 1 fat

Apple-Cheese Triangles

½ cup plus 1½ teaspoons margarine or butter, divided
¼ cup hazelnuts
1 large green or red cooking apple, cored and chopped
2 tablespoons lemon juice
2 tablespoons sugar
⅓ to ½ cup crumbled blue cheese
9 sheets frozen phyllo dough (18 x 14-inch sheets), defrosted

10 to 12 servings

Per Serving: Calories: 171 • Protein: 3 g.
• Carbohydrate: 16 g. • Fat: 11 g.
• Cholesterol: 4 mg. • Sodium: 224 mg.
Exchanges: ½ starch, ¼ high-fat meat, ½ fruit, 2 fat

How to Make Apple-Cheese Triangles

Place 1½ teaspoons margarine in 9-inch pie plate. Microwave at High for 30 to 45 seconds, or until melted. Stir in hazelnuts, tossing to coat.

Microwave at High for 5 to 6 minutes, or until browned, stirring every 2 minutes. Chop hazelnuts. Set aside. In 1½-quart casserole, combine apple, juice and sugar. Cover.

Microwave at High for 4 to 6 minutes, or until apple is tender, stirring once. Drain. Add cheese and hazelnuts. Stir until cheese is melted. Set aside.

Heat conventional oven to 400°F. In 2-cup measure, microwave remaining ½ cup margarine at High for 1½ to 1¾ minutes, or until melted. Place 1 sheet phyllo on flat surface. Quickly brush with margarine and layer on 2 more sheets, first brushing each with margarine.

Cut sheets in half lengthwise, then cut each half crosswise into 6 equal parts. Spoon heaping teaspoon of filling onto end of each strip. Fold lower right corner to opposite side, forming triangle. Continue folding until strip is used.

Repeat with remaining phyllo sheets, margarine and filling until filling is used up. Brush tops of triangles with any remaining margarine. Bake conventionally for 10 to 12 minutes, or until golden brown. Serve warm.

48

Savory Mushroom Tart

1 lb. mushrooms, trimmed
   and finely chopped
   (5 cups)
1/3 cup chopped shallots
1 tablespoon margarine or
   butter
2 teaspoons fresh thyme
   leaves
1 cup shredded spinach
   leaves
1/3 cup chopped red pepper
1 pkg. (8 oz.) cream cheese
1 pkg. (17 1/4 oz.) frozen puff
   pastry sheets, defrosted
1 egg yolk, beaten with
   1 tablespoon water

12 servings

Heat conventional oven to 350°F.
In 2-quart casserole, combine
mushrooms, shallots, margarine and thyme. Microwave at
High for 5 to 8 minutes, or until
mushrooms are tender, stirring
twice. Drain, pressing with back
of spoon to remove excess moisture. Add spinach and red pepper. Set aside.

In small mixing bowl, microwave
cream cheese at 50% (Medium)
for 1 1/2 to 3 minutes, or until
softened. Stir until smooth. Add
to mushroom mixture. Mix well.
Place 1 sheet puff pastry on
flat surface. Top with mushroom
mixture, spreading to within
1 inch of edge. Brush edge
with some of egg yolk mixture.
Top with remaining sheet of puff
pastry. Press edges to seal.
Score top with sharp knife in dia-
mond pattern by making 1/8-inch-
deep cuts at 1-inch intervals.
Bake conventionally for 35 to 45
minutes, or until puffed and deep
golden brown. Serve in squares.

Per Serving: Calories: 267 • Protein: 5 g.
• Carbohydrate: 18 g. • Fat: 19 g.
• Cholesterol: 39 mg. • Sodium: 268 mg.
Exchanges: 1 starch, 1/2 vegetable, 4 fat

Oriental Bow Ties with Pineapple Dip ▲

1 cup finely chopped
   pineapple
1/4 cup finely chopped red
   pepper
1/4 cup water
2 tablespoons sugar
1 tablespoon grated orange
   peel
1/4 teaspoon onion powder
2 teaspoons cornstarch
   mixed with 1 tablespoon
   water
18 eggroll skin strips
   (7 x 1-inch strips)*
   Vegetable oil

4 to 6 servings

In 1-quart casserole, combine all ingredients, except cornstarch
mixture, eggroll strips and oil. Cover. Microwave at High for 10 to 12
minutes, or until pepper is very tender, stirring once. Blend in cornstarch mixture. Microwave at High for 30 to 45 seconds, or until dip
is thickened and translucent, stirring once. Set aside.

Tie eggroll strips into loose knots. In 10-inch nonstick skillet, heat
1/4 inch oil conventionally over medium heat. Add knots, a few at a
time, to skillet. Cook for 15 to 30 seconds, or until golden brown on
both sides, turning over once. Drain on paper-towel-lined plate.
Serve with warm or chilled dip.

* Use eggroll skin trimmings from Spinach & Dill Turnovers, page 46,
or Potato & Chive Turnovers, page 47.

Per Serving: Calories: 88 • Protein: 1 g. • Carbohydrate: 15 g. • Fat: 3 g.
• Cholesterol: 8 mg. • Sodium: 3 mg.
Exchanges: 1/2 starch, 1/2 fruit, 1/2 fat

49

Fresh & Easy Soups

Chinese Vegetable Soup

2 cups shredded savoy cabbage
1 cup diagonally sliced snow pea pods
 (1-inch lengths)
1 cup chopped red peppers
4 oz. coarsely chopped enoki mushrooms
 (1 cup)
½ cup carrot strips (2 × ¼-inch strips)
½ cup sliced green onions
2 teaspoons sesame oil
2 tablespoons cornstarch
½ teaspoon anise seed
⅛ teaspoon cayenne
2 cans (14½ oz. each) ready-to-serve
 chicken broth

6 servings

In 3-quart casserole, combine cabbage, pea pods, red peppers, mushrooms, carrot, onions and oil. Cover. Microwave at High for 7 to 10 minutes, or until vegetables are tender-crisp, stirring once. In 4-cup measure, combine cornstarch, anise and cayenne. Blend in broth. Add to vegetable mixture. Re-cover. Microwave at High for 10 to 13 minutes, or until soup is slightly thickened and translucent, stirring once or twice.

Per Serving: Calories: 73 • Protein: 4 g. • Carbohydrate: 10 g.
• Fat: 3 g. • Cholesterol: 0 • Sodium: 609 mg.
Exchanges: 2 vegetable, ½ fat

Mexican Vegetable Salsa Soup

2 medium tomatoes, chopped (2 cups)
2 ears corn on the cob (8 to 10 oz. each),
 kernels sliced off (1½ cups) and cobs
 discarded
½ cup chopped red onion
1 jalapeño pepper, seeded and chopped
1 tablespoon vegetable oil
1 can (16 oz.) pinto beans, rinsed and
 drained
1 medium avocado, peeled and chopped
 (1 cup)
1 cup ready-to-serve chicken broth
2 tablespoons snipped fresh cilantro leaves
2 to 3 teaspoons chili powder
½ teaspoon ground cumin
½ teaspoon sugar

4 to 6 servings

In 2-quart casserole, combine tomatoes, corn, onion, jalapeño and oil. Cover. Microwave at High for 8 to 13 minutes, or until onion is tender, stirring once. Add remaining ingredients. Mix well. Re-cover. Microwave at High for 6 to 10 minutes, or until soup is hot and flavors are blended, stirring once.

Per Serving: Calories: 164 • Protein: 6 g. • Carbohydrate: 21 g.
• Fat: 8 g. • Cholesterol: 0 • Sodium: 313 mg.
Exchanges: 1 starch, 1 vegetable, 1½ fat

Indonesian Vegetable Chowder

1½ cups finely shredded red cabbage
  1 cup sliced green beans (¼-inch lengths)
½ cup diagonally sliced carrot
½ cup chopped onion
  1 tablespoon vegetable oil
  1 can (14½ oz.) ready-to-serve chicken broth
  1 cup water
  1 cup uncooked instant white rice
½ cup raisins
  1 teaspoon grated fresh gingerroot
½ teaspoon turmeric
¼ teaspoon ground cinnamon

4 servings

In 2-quart casserole, combine cabbage, beans, carrot, onion and oil. Cover. Microwave at High for 6 to 10 minutes, or until beans are tender-crisp, stirring once.

Add remaining ingredients. Mix well. Re-cover. Microwave at High for 8 to 10 minutes, or until vegetables are tender and flavors are blended, stirring once.

Per Serving: Calories: 218 • Protein: 5 g. • Carbohydrate: 42 g. • Fat: 4 g. • Cholesterol: 0 • Sodium: 461 mg.
Exchanges: 1 starch, 2½ vegetable, 1 fruit, ¾ fat

Cream of Three-Onion Soup

 1 cup sliced leek
 1 cup halved peeled white pearl onions
 1/2 cup sliced green onions
 2 tablespoons margarine or butter
 1/4 cup plus 2 tablespoons all-purpose flour
 1 tablespoon Dijon mustard
 1/4 teaspoon garlic powder
 1/8 teaspoon white pepper
 1 can (14 1/2 oz.) ready-to-serve chicken broth
 1 1/2 cups half-and-half or cream

4 to 6 servings

In 3-quart casserole, combine leek, onions and margarine. Cover. Microwave at High for 6 to 8 minutes, or until vegetables are tender, stirring once. Stir in flour, mustard, garlic powder and pepper. Blend in broth and half-and-half.

Microwave at 70% (Medium High), uncovered, for 10 to 13 minutes, or until soup thickens slightly and bubbles, stirring twice. (Do not boil.) Garnish with snipped fresh chives or green onion, if desired.

Per Serving: Calories: 177 • Protein: 4 g. • Carbohydrate: 15 g.
• Fat: 11 g. • Cholesterol: 22 mg. • Sodium: 450 mg.
Exchanges: 1/2 starch, 1 1/2 vegetable, 2 1/4 fat

Cream of Carrot Soup ▲

 1 lb. carrots, peeled and sliced (3 cups)
 1 cup ready-to-serve chicken broth, divided
 1/2 cup chopped onion
 2 tablespoons all-purpose flour
 1/8 teaspoon white pepper
 1 cup milk

4 servings

In 2-quart casserole, combine carrots, 1/4 cup broth and the onion. Cover. Microwave at High for 11 to 15 minutes, or until carrots are tender, stirring twice. In food processor or blender, process carrot mixture until smooth. Return purée to casserole.

In 2-cup measure, combine flour and pepper. Blend in remaining 3/4 cup broth. Add broth mixture to casserole. Microwave at High, uncovered, for 3 to 4 minutes, or until mixture is slightly thickened, stirring every minute. Stir in milk. Microwave at 70% (Medium High) for 3 to 4 minutes, or until soup is hot, stirring once. Garnish with croutons, if desired.

Per Serving: Calories: 109 • Protein: 4 g. • Carbohydrate: 18 g.
• Fat: 3 g. • Cholesterol: 9 mg. • Sodium: 313 mg.
Exchanges: 2 1/2 vegetable, 1/4 low-fat milk, 1/2 fat

Cream of Tomato-Basil Soup

1/3 cup chopped shallots
1 tablespoon olive oil
1 clove garlic, minced
1 can (28 oz.) Roma
  tomatoes, undrained and
  cut up
1/2 cup ready-to-serve chicken
  broth
1/4 cup snipped fresh basil
  leaves
1/2 teaspoon sugar
1/2 teaspoon freshly ground
  pepper
1/4 teaspoon salt
4 Roma tomatoes, chopped
  (2 cups), divided
1 cup half-and-half or cream,
  divided

6 servings

In 2-quart casserole, combine shallots, oil and garlic. Cover. Micro-wave at High for 2 to 3 minutes, or until tender. Add canned toma-toes, broth, basil, sugar, pepper and salt. Microwave at High, uncovered, for 4 to 6 minutes, or until mixture is hot and flavors are blended, stirring once.

In food processor or blender, combine half of tomato mixture, 2 Roma tomatoes and 1/2 cup half-and-half. Process until smooth. Set purée aside. Repeat with remaining ingredients. Return purée to casserole. Cover. Microwave at 70% (Medium High) for 13 to 15 minutes, or until soup is hot, stirring twice. Spoon into serving dishes. Top each serv-ing with 1 crostini*, if desired.

* To make crostini, arrange 6 thin slices Italian bread on baking sheet. Brush slices evenly with 1 tablespoon olive oil. Top each with 2 thin slices Roma tomato, 1 small fresh basil leaf and 1 teaspoon shredded fresh Parmesan cheese. Broil conventionally 5 inches from heat for 4 to 5 minutes, or until golden brown.

Per Serving: Calories: 117 • Protein: 3 g. • Carbohydrate: 11 g. • Fat: 7 g.
• Cholesterol: 15 mg. • Sodium: 408 mg.
Exchanges: 2 1/4 vegetable, 1 1/2 fat

◀ Spiced Tomato & Zucchini Soup

1 can (28 oz.) Roma
   tomatoes, undrained and
   cut up
2 medium tomatoes,
   chopped (2 cups)
1 medium zucchini, thinly
   sliced (1 cup)
2 ears corn on the cob (8 to
   10 oz. each), kernels sliced
   off (1½ cups) and cobs
   discarded
1 cup ready-to-serve chicken
   broth
1 tablespoon olive oil
1 tablespoon chili powder
½ teaspoon sugar
¼ teaspoon ground cinnamon

6 to 8 servings

In 3-quart casserole, combine
all ingredients. Cover. Microwave at High for 25 to 30 minutes, or until vegetables are
tender and flavors are blended,
stirring every 5 minutes.

Per Serving: Calories: 79 • Protein: 3 g.
• Carbohydrate: 13 g. • Fat: 3 g.
• Cholesterol: 0 • Sodium: 303 mg.
Exchanges: ¼ starch, 2 vegetable, ½ fat

Sweet Potato Vichyssoise

2 medium sweet potatoes,
   peeled and cut into ½-inch
   cubes (2 cups)
1 cup sliced leek
¼ cup dry white wine
2 tablespoons margarine or
   butter
1 teaspoon grated fresh
   gingerroot
1 cup ready-to-serve chicken
   broth
1 cup milk

4 servings

In 2-quart casserole, combine all ingredients, except broth and
milk. Cover. Microwave at High for 8 to 13 minutes, or until potatoes
are very tender, stirring once.

In food processor or blender, process potato mixture until smooth.
Return purée to casserole. Stir in broth and milk. Microwave at 70%
(Medium High), uncovered, for 8 to 10 minutes, or until soup is hot
and flavors are blended, stirring once. Serve hot or cold. Garnish
with snipped fresh chives, if desired.

Per Serving: Calories: 182 • Protein: 4 g. • Carbohydrate: 23 g. • Fat: 8 g.
• Cholesterol: 9 mg. • Sodium: 358 mg.
Exchanges: 1 starch, ½ vegetable, ¼ low-fat milk, 1¾ fat

Spicy Tortellini Stew ▲

8 oz. mushrooms, sliced (2 cups)
1 cup chopped onions
1 tablespoon olive oil
1 clove garlic, minced
2 medium tomatoes, chopped (2 cups)
1 can (14½ oz.) ready-to-serve beef broth
1 can (8 oz.) tomato sauce
½ cup thick and chunky salsa
2 tablespoons snipped fresh basil leaves
1 pkg. (9 oz.) uncooked fresh cheese tortellini

6 servings

In 3-quart casserole, combine mushrooms, onions, oil and garlic. Cover. Microwave at High for 8 to 10 minutes, or just until mushrooms are tender, stirring once.

Add remaining ingredients, except tortellini. Mix well. Re-cover. Microwave at High for 10 to 12 minutes, or until mixture is hot and flavors are blended, stirring once. Add tortellini. Re-cover. Microwave at High for 10 to 15 minutes, or until tortellini are tender, stirring once. Sprinkle with shredded fresh Parmesan cheese, if desired.

Per Serving: Calories: 204 • Protein: 10 g. • Carbohydrate: 32 g. • Fat: 5 g. • Cholesterol: 23 mg. • Sodium: 797 mg.
Exchanges: 1¼ starch, ¼ lean meat, 2½ vegetable, ¾ fat

Ratatouille Soup

1 medium eggplant (1 lb.), peeled and cut into 1-inch cubes
1 cup chopped onions
2 tablespoons olive oil
1 tablespoon snipped fresh rosemary
1 tablespoon lemon juice
1 to 2 cloves garlic, minced
1 can (28 oz.) Roma tomatoes, undrained and cut up
1 medium zucchini, sliced (1 cup)
1 cup chopped green peppers
4 oz. mushrooms, sliced (1 cup)
1 cup ready-to-serve chicken broth
¼ to ½ teaspoon freshly ground pepper

8 servings

In 3-quart casserole, combine eggplant, onions, oil, rosemary, juice and garlic. Cover. Microwave at High for 10 to 15 minutes, or until eggplant is tender, stirring twice.

Add remaining ingredients. Mix well. Re-cover. Microwave at High for 18 to 21 minutes, or until vegetables are tender, stirring twice.

Per Serving: Calories: 84 • Protein: 3 g. • Carbohydrate: 11 g. • Fat: 4 g. • Cholesterol: 0 • Sodium: 289 mg.
Exchanges: 2¼ vegetable, ⅔ fat

Mushroom Ham Soup

4   cups sliced mixed mushrooms (shiitake,
     chanterelle, crimini, white button)
¼   cup dry sherry
3   cups hot water
½   cup fully cooked lean ham strips
     (2 × ¼-inch strips)
½   cup diagonally sliced green onions (1-inch
     lengths)
3   teaspoons instant beef bouillon granules
½   teaspoon sugar
     Dash freshly ground pepper

4 to 5 servings

In 3-quart casserole, combine mushrooms and
sherry. Cover. Microwave at High for 4 to 5 minutes, or just until mushrooms are tender, stirring
once. Add remaining ingredients. Mix well. Re-
cover. Microwave at High for 4 to 6 minutes, or
until soup is hot and flavors are blended, stirring once.

Per Serving: Calories: 61 • Protein: 5 g. • Carbohydrate: 6 g.
• Fat: 1 g. • Cholesterol: 7 mg. • Sodium: 678 mg.
Exchanges: ½ lean meat, ½ vegetable, ¼ fruit

Caribbean Onion Chili

1   medium sweet potato, peeled and cut into
     ½-inch cubes (1 cup)
½   cup chopped onion
1   Anaheim pepper, seeded and chopped
     (½ cup)
1   tablespoon peanut oil or vegetable oil
2   cups hot water
1   can (16 oz.) Great Northern beans, rinsed
     and drained
1   cup cooked long-grain white rice
2   tablespoons red wine vinegar
1   tablespoon packed brown sugar
2   teaspoons instant chicken bouillon granules
     Dash freshly ground pepper

4 servings

In 2-quart casserole, combine potato, onion,
Anaheim pepper and oil. Cover. Microwave at
High for 6 to 8 minutes, or until potato is tender-
crisp, stirring once. Add remaining ingredients.
Mix well. Re-cover. Microwave at High for 5 to 8
minutes, or until vegetables are tender, stirring
once. Garnish with sliced green onions, if desired.

Per Serving: Calories: 226 • Protein: 7 g. • Carbohydrate: 40 g.
• Fat: 4 g. • Cholesterol: 0 • Sodium: 672 mg.
Exchanges: 2½ starch, ¾ fat

Split Pea Sage Soup ▲

  1 cup dried yellow or green split peas, rinsed and drained

  1 can (14½ oz.) ready-to-serve chicken broth

  2 to 3 tablespoons snipped fresh sage leaves

3¼ cups water, divided

  4 red potatoes, cut into ½-inch cubes (2 cups)

  1 cup coarsely chopped carrots

  ½ teaspoon freshly ground pepper

  ¼ teaspoon salt

4 to 6 servings

In 2-quart casserole, combine peas, broth and sage. Cover. Microwave at High for 8 to 10 minutes, or until boiling, stirring once. Let stand, covered, for 1 hour.

In 1½-quart casserole, combine ¼ cup water, the potatoes and carrots. Cover. Microwave at High for 10 to 12 minutes, or until potato is tender-crisp, stirring once. Drain.

In 6-quart Dutch oven, combine pea mixture, remaining 3 cups water, the potato mixture and remaining ingredients. Bring to a boil conventionally over medium heat, stirring frequently. Reduce heat to low. Simmer soup, partially covered, for 45 minutes to 1 hour, or until peas are tender, stirring occasionally.

Per Serving: Calories: 169 • Protein: 10 g. • Carbohydrate: 31 g. • Fat: 1 g.
• Cholesterol: 0 • Sodium: 403 mg.
Exchanges: 2 starch

Pepper & Cheese Bisque

3 cups chopped red, green and yellow peppers
1 cup sliced celery
1 red chili pepper or jalapeño pepper, sliced and seeded
2 tablespoons margarine or butter
1/4 cup all-purpose flour
1 teaspoon instant chicken bouillon granules
1/2 teaspoon celery salt
3 cups milk
1 cup shredded Cheddar cheese or pasteurized process American cheese loaf

6 servings

In 3-quart casserole, combine peppers, celery, chili pepper and margarine. Cover. Microwave at High for 10 to 12 minutes, or until vegetables are tender, stirring once. Stir in flour, bouillon and salt. Blend in milk. Microwave at High, uncovered, for 6 to 8 minutes, or until bisque is slightly thickened, stirring every 2 minutes. Stir in cheese until melted.

Per Serving: Calories: 222 • Protein: 10 g. • Carbohydrate: 14 g. • Fat: 14 g.
• Cholesterol: 37 mg. • Sodium: 520 mg.
Exchanges: 1/4 starch, 3/4 high-fat meat, 1 vegetable, 1/2 low-fat milk, 1 1/2 fat

Spinach Bisque

1 cup sliced celery
1/3 to 1/2 cup sliced green onions
1 tablespoon olive oil
1 clove garlic, minced
3 tablespoons all-purpose flour
3 cups milk
3 tablespoons tomato paste
1/4 teaspoon salt
1/8 teaspoon cayenne
3 cups shredded spinach leaves

4 servings

In 2-quart casserole, combine celery, onions, oil and garlic. Cover. Microwave at High for 4 to 6 minutes, or until celery is tender, stirring once. Stir in flour. Blend in milk. Microwave at High, uncovered, for 8 to 13 minutes, or until mixture is slightly thickened, stirring every 2 minutes.

Using wire whisk, blend in tomato paste, salt and cayenne. Add spinach. Cover. Microwave at High for 1 to 2 minutes, or until spinach is wilted.

NOTE: If desired, add 1 can (6 oz.) crab meat, rinsed and drained, with spinach.

Per Serving: Calories: 192 • Protein: 9 g. • Carbohydrate: 19 g. • Fat: 10 g.
• Cholesterol: 26 mg. • Sodium: 383 mg.
Exchanges: 2 vegetable, 3/4 low-fat milk, 2 fat

Vegetable Gumbo ▶

1/4 cup all-purpose flour
1 can (14 1/2 oz.) ready-to-serve chicken broth, divided
1 medium zucchini squash, sliced (1 cup)
1 medium yellow squash, sliced (1 cup)
1 ear corn on the cob (8 to 10 oz.), kernels sliced off (3/4 cup) and cob discarded
1/2 cup chopped peeled kohlrabi
1/2 cup chopped peeled carrot
1/2 cup sliced leek
2 medium tomatoes, chopped (2 cups)
1 cup sliced okra (1/2-inch slices)
1/4 teaspoon freshly ground pepper
Hot cooked rice

4 to 5 servings

Heat conventional oven to 400°F. Sprinkle flour evenly into 8-inch square baking pan. Bake for 10 to 15 minutes, or until flour is deep golden brown, stirring every 5 minutes. Set aside.

In 3-quart casserole, combine 1/4 cup broth, the squashes, corn, kohlrabi, carrot and leek. Cover. Microwave at High for 11 to 15 minutes, or until zucchini is tender, stirring once.

Stir in flour. Blend in remaining broth. Add tomatoes, okra and pepper. Mix well. Re-cover. Microwave at High for 15 to 20 minutes, or until gumbo is slightly thickened and vegetables are tender, stirring 3 times. Serve over hot cooked rice.

Per Serving: Calories: 99 • Protein: 4 g.
• Carbohydrate: 20 g. • Fat: 1 g.
• Cholesterol: 0 • Sodium: 379 mg.
Exchanges: 1/2 starch, 2 1/2 vegetable

Sweet & Sour Pineapple Soup

- 1 cup red and green pepper strips (2 × ¼-inch strips)
- 1 cup sliced leek
- 1 tablespoon water
- 2 tablespoons cornstarch
- 2 tablespoons packed brown sugar
- ¼ teaspoon crushed red pepper flakes
- 2 cans (14½ oz. each) ready-to-serve chicken broth
- 2 tablespoons white vinegar
- 2 cups pineapple chunks (½-inch chunks)

6 servings

Per Serving: Calories: 85 • Protein: 2 g.
• Carbohydrate: 18 g. • Fat: 1 g.
• Cholesterol: 0 • Sodium: 602 mg.
Exchanges: 1 vegetable, 1 fruit

How to Microwave Sweet & Sour Pineapple Soup

Combine peppers, leek and water in 3-quart casserole. Cover. Microwave at High for 4 to 6 minutes, or until peppers are tender-crisp, stirring once. Set aside.

Combine cornstarch, sugar and red pepper flakes in 4-cup measure. Blend in broth and vinegar. Add broth mixture and pineapple to casserole. Mix well. Re-cover. Microwave at High for 10 to 15 minutes, or until soup is slightly thickened and translucent, stirring every 5 minutes.

Pumpkin Soup

1 small pumpkin (2 lbs.), peeled, seeded
   and cut into 1-inch cubes
1 can (5½ oz.) apricot nectar
½ cup sliced green onions
1 tablespoon margarine or butter
½ teaspoon grated fresh orange peel
¼ to ½ teaspoon grated fresh gingerroot
¼ teaspoon ground nutmeg
¼ teaspoon salt
¼ teaspoon freshly ground pepper
1 cup milk

4 servings

In 3-quart casserole, combine pumpkin and
nectar. Cover. Microwave at High for 13 to 15
minutes, or until pumpkin is tender, stirring twice.
In food processor or blender, process pumpkin
mixture until smooth. Set aside.

In same casserole, combine onions and margarine. Cover. Microwave at High for 2 to 3 minutes,
or until onions are tender-crisp, stirring once.
Add pumpkin purée and remaining ingredients,
except milk, to casserole. Re-cover.

Microwave at High for 4 to 5 minutes, or until mixture is hot and
bubbly, stirring once. Stir in milk.
Re-cover. Microwave at High for
2 to 3 minutes, or until soup is hot.
Garnish with toasted pumpkin
seeds*, if desired.

* To make toasted pumpkin seeds,
save ½ cup seeds from pumpkin.
Heat conventional oven to 300°F.
Rinse, drain and pat seeds dry.
In small mixing bowl, combine
seeds, 1 teaspoon vegetable oil
and ½ teaspoon seasoned salt.
Spread seeds in single layer on
baking sheet. Bake for 25 to 28
minutes, or until golden brown,
stirring every 10 minutes.

Per Serving: Calories: 134 • Protein: 4 g.
• Carbohydrate: 21 g. • Fat: 5 g.
• Cholesterol: 9 mg. • Sodium: 203 mg.
Exchanges: 1 starch, ½ vegetable,
¼ low-fat milk, 1 fat

Fall Fruit Gazpacho ▼

2 cups apple juice
½ cup orange juice
½ cup golden raisins
½ cup snipped dried apricots
2 tablespoons packed brown sugar
2 tablespoons lemon juice
1 small stick cinnamon
4 cups chopped mixed fruits (apple, pear,
   peach, grapes, figs)

5 to 6 servings

In 2-quart casserole, combine all ingredients,
except chopped fruits. Microwave at High, uncovered, for 7 to 9 minutes, or until mixture is
hot and raisins are plumped. Discard cinnamon
stick. Add fruits. Mix well. Cool slightly. Cover
and chill.

Per Serving: Calories: 178 • Protein: 1 g. • Carbohydrate: 46 g.
• Fat: 0 • Cholesterol: 0 • Sodium: 8 mg.
Exchanges: 3 fruit

Tangy Grilled Chicken Salad

  2 boneless whole chicken breasts (8 to 10 oz. each), split in half, skin removed
 ¼ teaspoon salt
 ¼ teaspoon freshly ground pepper

Dressing:

 ⅓ cup white wine vinegar
 ⅓ cup sliced green onions
  2 tablespoons olive oil
  2 tablespoons snipped watercress leaves

  1 medium red eating apple, cored and cut into 20 wedges
     Mixed salad greens, torn into bite-size pieces

4 servings

Sprinkle both sides of chicken evenly with salt and pepper. Grill chicken conventionally over medium-high heat for 18 to 20 minutes, or until meat is no longer pink and juices run clear, turning once.

Meanwhile, in 2-cup measure, combine all dressing ingredients, except watercress. Cover with plastic wrap. Microwave at High for 2 to 3 minutes, or until hot. Stir in watercress. Place apple wedges in medium mixng bowl. Add dressing. Toss to coat. Set aside.

Cut each breast half crosswise into 6 pieces. Arrange chicken on serving plates lined with mixed salad greens. Place apple wedges between chicken pieces. Pour dressing evenly over salads. Garnish with additional sliced green onions, if desired.

Per Serving: Calories: 222 • Protein: 26 g.
• Carbohydrate: 7 g. • Fat: 10 g.
• Cholesterol: 70 mg. • Sodium: 198 mg.
Exchanges: 3 lean meat, ½ fruit

Hearty Rice & Chicken Salad

  5 cups water
1½ cups uncooked wild rice
1¼ teaspoons salt, divided
  2 teaspoons olive oil
  1 clove garlic, minced
  ¼ teaspoon freshly ground pepper
  6 boneless skinless chicken thighs (2 to 3 oz.
     each), cut into 2 x ¼-inch strips
  2 cups whole strawberries, hulled and
     cut lengthwise into quarters
  1 medium avocado, peeled and cut into
     ½-inch cubes (1 cup)

Dressing:

  1 tablespoon grated orange peel
  ½ cup orange juice
  3 tablespoons olive oil
  2 tablespoons finely chopped walnuts
  1 tablespoon snipped fresh oregano leaves

6 servings

In 2-quart saucepan, combine water, rice and 1 teaspoon salt. Cook conventionally over medium-high heat until boiling. Cover. Reduce heat to low. Cook for 45 to 50 minutes longer, or until rice kernels are open. Drain. Place rice in large mixing bowl or salad bowl. Set aside.

In small bowl, combine remaining ¼ teaspoon salt, the oil, garlic and pepper. Place chicken in 8-inch square baking dish. Add seasoning mixture. Stir to coat. Cover with wax paper or microwave cooking paper. Microwave at High for 5 to 7 minutes, or until meat is no longer pink, stirring once. Drain. Add chicken, strawberries and avocado to rice. Stir to combine.

In 2-cup measure, combine dressing ingredients. Add to rice mixture. Toss to coat. Chill, if desired. Serve on lettuce-lined plates.

Per Serving: Calories: 469 • Protein: 20 g. • Carbohydrate: 41g.
• Fat: 26 g. • Cholesterol: 60 mg. • Sodium: 518 mg.
Exchanges: 1¾ starch, 2 lean meat, ½ vegetable, ¾ fruit, 4 fat

Pork & Peanut Potato Salad

Dressing:

2 teaspoons finely chopped
   seeded jalapeño pepper
2 teaspoons finely chopped
   peeled fresh gingerroot
1 teaspoon peanut oil
1/2 cup tomato juice
1/4 cup creamy peanut butter
1 tablespoon soy sauce

4 medium sweet potatoes,
   peeled and cut into 1/2-inch
   cubes (4 cups)
1/4 cup water
2/3 cup diagonally sliced
   green onions
   (1-inch lengths)
1 - lb. well-trimmed pork
   tenderloin, cut into
   2 × 1/4-inch strips
2 medium bananas, cut into
   1/4-inch slices (1 1/2 cups)

4 servings

In 2-cup measure, combine jalapeño pepper, gingerroot and oil. Microwave at High for 1 to 1 1/2 minutes, or until pepper is tender-crisp, stirring once. Stir in remaining dressing ingredients. Microwave at High for 30 seconds to 1 minute, or until hot. Whisk until smooth. Set aside.

In 2-quart casserole, combine potatoes and water. Cover. Microwave at High for 8 to 10 minutes, or until tender, stirring once. Drain. Place potatoes in large mixing bowl or salad bowl. Stir in onions. Cover with plastic wrap to keep warm. Set aside.

Wipe out casserole with paper towels. In same casserole, combine pork and 3 tablespoons dressing. Cover with wax paper or microwave cooking paper. Microwave at High for 4 to 6 minutes, or until meat is no longer pink, stirring once. Drain. Add pork and remaining dressing to potato mixture. Toss to combine. Stir in bananas. Serve on bed of shredded red or green cabbage. Sprinkle with dry-roasted peanuts, if desired.

Per Serving: Calories: 417 • Protein: 32 g. • Carbohydrate: 46 g. • Fat: 13 g.
• Cholesterol: 74 mg. • Sodium: 517 mg.
Exchanges: 1 1/2 starch, 3 1/4 lean meat, 1 3/4 vegetable, 1 fruit, 1/2 fat

Chicken Salad
with Watercress-Chèvre Dressing

Dressing:

- 4 oz. chèvre cheese (goat cheese)
- 2 tablespoons finely chopped shallots
- 2 tablespoons snipped watercress leaves
- 2 tablespoons olive oil
- 1 tablespoon white wine vinegar
- 1 teaspoon sugar
- 1/4 teaspoon salt

- 5 oz. baby carrots (1 cup)
- 1 tablespoon water
- 1 boneless whole chicken breast (8 to 10 oz.), split in half, skin removed
- 1/4 teaspoon seasoned salt
- 1/4 teaspoon freshly ground pepper
- 8 cups torn exotic salad green mix*

4 servings

In food processor or blender, combine dressing ingredients. Process until smooth. Cover with plastic wrap. Chill. In 1-quart casserole, combine carrots and water. Cover. Microwave at High for 3 to 4 minutes, or until tender-crisp, stirring once. Drain. Chill.

Sprinkle chicken evenly with salt and pepper. Place in 8-inch square baking dish. Cover with wax paper or microwave cooking paper. Microwave at High for 4 to 6 minutes, or until meat is no longer pink and juices run clear, rearranging once. Cool slightly. Slice into thin strips. Chill.

Arrange greens evenly on serving plates. Top evenly with carrots, chicken strips and dressing. Serve with crisp baguette rounds, if desired.

*Exotic salad green mix may contain: lollo rosso, red oak leaf, baby lettuce, radicchio, spinach, frisée, mâche, red mustard, arugula or chervil.

Per Serving: Calories: 267
• Protein: 21 g. • Carbohydrate: 9 g.
• Fat: 17 g. • Cholesterol: 58 mg.
• Sodium: 431 mg.
Exchanges: 2½ meat, 1¾ vegetable, 1 fat

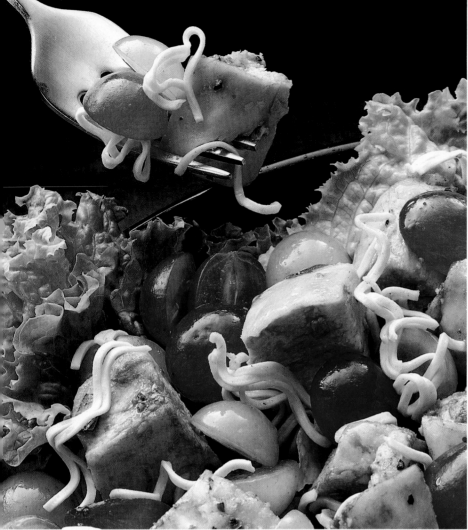

Pasta Puttanesca Salad

Dressing:
1 cup chopped onion
1 tablespoon olive oil
1 clove garlic, minced
1 can (15 oz.) tomato sauce
3 tablespoons snipped fresh oregano leaves or Italian parsley leaves
3 anchovy fillets, drained and mashed
2 tablespoons capers, rinsed and drained

½ teaspoon sugar
¼ teaspoon crushed red pepper flakes

8 oz. uncooked rotini pasta (2½ cups)
2 cups halved cherry tomatoes
½ cup halved pitted medium black olives

4 to 5 servings

In 1½-quart casserole, combine onion, oil and garlic. Microwave at High for 4 to 6 minutes, or until onion is tender, stirring once. Stir in remaining dressing ingredients. Cover. Microwave at High for 2 to 3 minutes, or until hot. Set aside.

Prepare pasta as directed on package. Rinse with cold water. Drain. Place in large mixing bowl or salad bowl. Stir in tomatoes and olives. Add dressing. Toss to coat. Cover with plastic wrap. Chill.

Per Serving: Calories: 264 • Protein: 9 g. • Carbohydrate: 46 g. • Fat: 5 g.
• Cholesterol: 1 mg. • Sodium: 816 mg.
Exchanges: 2 starch, 2 vegetable, 1 fat

◀ Tarragon Chicken Salad

Dressing:
¼ cup balsamic vinegar
2 tablespoons olive oil
1 tablespoon snipped fresh tarragon leaves
2 teaspoons packed brown sugar

2 boneless whole chicken breasts (8 to 10 oz. each), split in half, skin removed
2 teaspoons olive oil
1 clove garlic, minced
¼ teaspoon seasoned salt
¼ teaspoon freshly ground pepper
1 cup halved seedless green grapes
1 cup halved seedless red grapes
1 pkg. (3 oz.) Ramen soup mix (discard seasoning packet)

4 to 6 servings

In 1-cup measure, combine dressing ingredients. Set aside. Place chicken in 8-inch square baking dish. Add oil, garlic, salt and pepper. Turn to coat. Cover with wax paper or microwave cooking paper. Microwave at High for 4 to 9 minutes, or until meat is no longer pink and juices run clear. Cool slightly. Cut into ¾-inch pieces.

In large mixing bowl or salad bowl, combine chicken and grapes. Add dressing. Toss to coat. Cover with plastic wrap. Chill, stirring ocasionally. Just before serving, coarsely crush noodles. Add to salad. Toss to combine.

Per Serving: Calories: 242 • Protein: 19 g.
• Carbohydrate: 17 g. • Fat: 11g.
• Cholesterol: 47 mg. • Sodium: 180 mg.
Exchanges: ¼ starch, 2 lean meat, 1 fruit, 1 fat

Sweet & Sour Ham Salad

Dressing:
- ½ cup orange marmalade
- 2 tablespoons red wine vinegar
- ⅛ teaspoon salt
  Dash white pepper
- 1½ teaspoons cornstarch mixed with 2 teaspoons water

- 4 cups hot water
- 2 cups broccoli flowerets
- 2 cups shredded carrots
- 2 cups cauliflowerets
- 1½ cups cubed fully cooked lean ham (¾-inch cubes)
- 1 cup thinly sliced radishes

6 servings

In 2-cup measure, combine all dressing ingredients, except cornstarch mixture. Microwave at High for 2 to 3 minutes, or until mixture is hot and marmalade is melted. Stir in cornstarch mixture. Microwave at High for 30 seconds to 1 minute, or until dressing is thickened and translucent, stirring every 30 seconds. Cool slightly. Cover with plastic wrap. Chill.

Place water in 8-cup measure. Cover with plastic wrap. Microwave at High for 10 to 12 minutes, or until boiling. Plunge broccoli into boiling water for 30 seconds, or until color brightens. Using slotted spoon, remove broccoli and immediately plunge into ice water. Drain.

In large mixing bowl or salad bowl, combine broccoli and remaining ingredients. Add dressing. Toss to coat. Chill. Garnish with cashews, if desired.

Per Serving: Calories: 176 • Protein: 11 g. • Carbohydrate: 28 g. • Fat: 4 g.
• Cholesterol: 21 mg. • Sodium: 623 mg.
Exchanges: 1¼ lean meat, 1½ vegetable, 1¼ fruit

Asparagus Timbales

4 oz. asparagus tips*, ¾-inch
   lengths (1 cup)
2 tablespoons water
2 eggs, beaten
⅓ cup milk
3 tablespoons shredded
   Swiss cheese
2 tablespoons unseasoned
   dry bread crumbs
2 tablespoons finely
   chopped shallots
1 teaspoon grated lemon peel
¼ teaspoon salt
⅛ to ¼ teaspoon freshly
   ground pepper
   Paprika
   Boiling water

4 servings

*Use remaining spears in
Asparagus Guacamole,
page 33.

Per Serving: Calories: 92 • Protein: 7 g.
• Carbohydrate: 6 g. • Fat: 5 g.
• Cholesterol: 114 mg. • Sodium: 214 mg.
Exchanges: ¾ meat, 1 vegetable, ¼ fat

How to Microwave Asparagus Timbales

Combine asparagus tips and
2 tablespoons water in 1½-quart
casserole. Cover. Microwave at
High for 7 to 8 minutes, or until
tender, stirring once. Drain. Stir
in remaining ingredients, except paprika and boiling water.
Mix well.

Spray four ⅔-cup custard cups
with nonstick vegetable cooking
spray. Spoon asparagus mixture evenly into cups. Sprinkle
tops lightly with paprika. Arrange
cups in 10-inch square baking
dish. Pour boiling water into dish
around cups to ½-inch depth.

Microwave at 50% (Medium)
for 14 to 18 minutes, or until
wooden pick inserted in center
of timbales comes out clean,
rotating dish ¼ turn every 4 minutes. Let stand for 5 minutes.

Run thin-bladed knife around
edges and turn out timbales. If
desired, garnish with pimiento
slices and sprinkle with mixture of unseasoned dry bread
crumbs and melted margarine.

All-Vegetable Stir-fry Salad

- 1 medium red pepper, cut into 1-inch chunks (1½ cups)
- 1 small red onion, thinly sliced into rings
- 5 oz. baby carrots (1 cup), cut lengthwise into quarters
- 1 cup snow pea pods
- 2 tablespoons water
- 4 oz. mushrooms, sliced (1 cup)
- 1 can (8 oz.) sliced water chestnuts, rinsed and drained

Dressing:
- ¼ cup vegetable oil
- 3 tablespoons soy sauce
- 2 tablespoons rice wine vinegar
- 2 tablespoons sugar
- 1 tablespoon sesame seed
- ¼ teaspoon five-spice powder

- 6 cups shredded iceberg lettuce

5 servings

In 10-inch square casserole, combine red pepper, onion, carrots, pea pods and water. Cover. Microwave at High for 7 to 9 minutes, or until vegetables are tender-crisp, stirring once. Drain. Stir in mushrooms and water chestnuts. Cover. Set aside.

In 1-cup measure, combine dressing ingredients. Add dressing to vegetable mixture. Toss to coat. Re-cover. Microwave at High for 2 to 3 minutes, or until hot. Place lettuce in large mixing bowl or salad bowl. Add vegetable mixture to lettuce. Toss to combine. Serve immediately.

Per Serving: Calories: 201 • Protein: 4 g.
• Carbohydrate: 22 g. • Fat: 12 g.
• Cholesterol: 0 • Sodium: 641 mg.
Exchanges: 3 vegetable, ⅓ fruit, 2½ fat

Crab Gazpacho Salad ▲

Dressing:
- 1 cup Virgin Mary, page 29, or spicy vegetable juice
- ½ cup finely chopped cucumber
- ½ cup finely chopped green pepper
- ⅓ cup finely chopped red onion
- ¼ cup olive oil
- 2 tablespoons red wine vinegar
- ½ teaspoon red pepper sauce (optional)

- 1 pkg. (16 oz.) uncooked bow-tie pasta
- 3 medium tomatoes, seeded and chopped (3 cups)
- 8 oz. imitation crab meat, cut into ½-inch diagonal pieces
- 1 cup sliced celery

8 servings

In 4-cup measure, combine dressing ingredients. Set aside. Prepare pasta as directed on package. Rinse with cold water. Drain. Place in large mixing bowl or salad bowl. Stir in remaining ingredients. Add dressing. Toss to coat. Chill.

Serve on lettuce-lined plates. Garnish with snipped fresh parsley, sliced green onions or Greek olives, if desired.

Per Serving: Calories: 323 • Protein: 11 g. • Carbohydrate: 52 g. • Fat: 9 g.
• Cholesterol: 4 mg. • Sodium: 334 mg.
Exchanges: 2½ starch, 2 vegetable, 1 fat

Breakfast Fruit Salad

1 large grapefruit (1½ lbs.), peeled and sectioned
¼ cup sugar
1 tablespoon plus 1 teaspoon cornstarch mixed with 1 tablespoon water
5 plums, pitted and each cut into 8 wedges
5 apricots, peeled*, pitted and each cut into 8 wedges

4 servings

Peel away and discard membrane from grapefruit segments. Place grapefruit in 1½-quart casserole. Stir in sugar. Cover. Microwave at High for 4 to 5 minutes, or until sugar is dissolved and mixture is hot, stirring once.

Strain mixture through sieve into 4-cup measure, pressing with back of spoon to release juice. Discard pulp. Microwave juice at High for 2 to 3 minutes, or just until boiling. Stir in cornstarch mixture. Microwave at High for 30 seconds, or until dressing is thickened and translucent, stirring once. Set aside.

In large mixing bowl or salad bowl, combine plums and apricots. Add dressing. Toss to coat. Chill. Serve on lettuce-lined plates. Sprinkle with brown sugar and garnish with lime zest, if desired.

Per Serving: Calories: 152 • Protein: 2 g.
• Carbohydrate: 37 g. • Fat: 1 g.
• Cholesterol: 0 • Sodium: 1 mg.
Exchanges: 2½ fruit

*How to Peel Apricots

Place 4 cups hot water in 8-cup measure. Cover with plastic wrap.

Microwave at High for 10 to 12 minutes, or until boiling. Immerse apricots in water for 1 to 2 minutes to loosen skins.

Remove apricots with slotted spoon and immerse in cold water. Peel and discard skins.

Peachy Turkey Salad

2 turkey tenderloins (8 to 10 oz. each)
1/4 teaspoon salt
1/4 teaspoon freshly ground pepper

Dressing:

1/4 cup vegetable oil
2 tablespoons orange juice
2 tablespoons lime juice
1 tablespoon sugar
1 tablespoon fresh thyme leaves

5 small peaches, peeled* and cut into thin wedges
1/4 cup chopped pecans
1/3 cup crumbled Gorgonzola or blue cheese

4 servings

Sprinkle turkey evenly with salt and pepper. Place in 8-inch square baking dish. Cover with wax paper or microwave cooking paper. Microwave at High for 8 to 10 minutes, or until meat is no longer pink and juices run clear, rearranging once. Drain. Cool slightly. Cut into 3/4-inch pieces. Set aside.

In 2-cup measure, combine dressing ingredients. Stir until sugar is dissolved. In large mixing bowl or salad bowl, combine turkey, peaches and pecans. Add dressing. Toss to coat. Stir in cheese. Serve on lettuce-lined plates. Top with additional cheese, if desired.

*See How to Peel Apricots, opposite.

Per Serving: Calories: 422 • Protein: 35 g. • Carbohydrate: 21 g. • Fat: 22 g. • Cholesterol: 87 mg. • Sodium: 355 mg.
Exchanges: 5 lean meat, 1 1/2 fruit, 1 1/2 fat

Fruited Tabbouleh

1¼ cups hot water
¾ cup uncooked bulgur
(cracked wheat)
2 medium seedless
oranges, peeled and
sectioned
½ cup raspberries
¼ cup chopped pecans

Dressing:
¼ cup vegetable oil
3 tablespoons red wine
vinegar
2 tablespoons frozen orange
juice concentrate,
defrosted
¼ teaspoon ground cinnamon
⅛ teaspoon ground allspice

Leaf lettuce

6 servings

Place water in 1½-quart casserole. Cover. Microwave at High
for 4 to 6 minutes, or until boiling. Stir in bulgur. Re-cover. Let
stand for 15 to 20 minutes, or
until liquid is absorbed. Fluff
with fork. Add oranges, raspberries and pecans. Stir to combine. Set aside.

In 1-cup measure, combine
dressing ingredients. Pour dressing over salad. Toss to coat.
Cover with plastic wrap. Chill.
Serve on lettuce-lined plates.

Per Serving: Calories: 209 • Protein: 3 g.
• Carbohydrate: 24 g. • Fat: 13 g.
• Cholesterol: 0 • Sodium: 3 mg.
Exchanges: ¾ starch, ¾ fruit, 2½ fat

Orange-Sprout Salad

1 medium cucumber, cut in
half lengthwise and sliced
(2 cups)
1 cup thinly sliced radishes
1 cup bean sprouts
1 cup alfalfa sprouts

Dressing:
2 tablespoons honey
1 tablespoon grated orange
peel
1 tablespoon orange juice

Sorrel leaves

4 servings

In large mixing bowl or salad
bowl, combine cucumber,
radishes and sprouts. Set aside.
In 1-cup measure, combine
dressing ingredients. Microwave
at High for 30 seconds to 1½
minutes, or until hot, stirring
once. Pour over cucumber mixture, tossing to coat. Serve on
sorrel-lined plates.

Per Serving: Calories: 58 • Protein: 2 g.
• Carbohydrate: 14 g. • Fat: 0
• Cholesterol: 0 • Sodium: 11 mg.
Exchanges: 1½ vegetable, ½ fruit

Fennel & Orange Salad ▶

1½ teaspoons margarine or butter
¼ cup sliced almonds
2 medium seedless oranges, peeled and thinly sliced
1 bulb fennel (8 to 10 oz.), cut into ¼-inch wedges and separated
4 oz. cooked smoked turkey breast, cut into 2 × ¼-inch strips (optional)

Dressing:

2 tablespoons olive oil
2 tablespoons red wine vinegar
1 tablespoon snipped fresh tarragon leaves
1 teaspoon sugar

Leaf lettuce

4 servings

In 9-inch pie plate, microwave margarine at High for 30 to 45 seconds, or until melted. Stir in almonds, tossing to coat. Microwave at High for 4 to 5 minutes, or until golden brown, stirring every 2 minutes. Set aside.

In large mixing bowl or salad bowl, combine oranges, fennel and turkey. In 1-cup measure, combine dressing ingredients. Add to orange mixture. Toss to coat. Serve on lettuce-lined plates. Garnish evenly with toasted almonds.

Per Serving: Calories: 157 • Protein: 2 g.
• Carbohydrate: 13 g. • Fat: 11 g.
• Cholesterol: 0 • Sodium: 75 mg.
Exchanges: 1 vegetable, ½ fruit, 2¼ fat

Hot Apple & Pear Waldorf Salad

2 medium d'Anjou pears, cored and cut into ½-inch cubes
1 medium red cooking apple, cored and cut into ½-inch cubes
2 tablespoons lemon juice
1 bulb fennel (8 to 10 oz.), cut in half lengthwise and sliced
½ cup chopped walnuts
½ cup raisins

Dressing:

⅓ cup mayonnaise
2 tablespoons apple cider
¼ teaspoon ground cinnamon

6 servings

In 2-quart casserole, combine pears, apple and juice. Cover. Microwave at High for 5 to 6 minutes, or until fruit is tender-crisp, stirring once. Drain. Stir in fennel, walnuts and raisins.

In small mixing bowl, combine dressing ingredients. Add to salad. Toss to coat. Serve warm. Garnish with additional apple and pear slices, if desired.

Per Serving: Calories: 243 • Protein: 3 g.
• Carbohydrate: 26 g. • Fat: 16 g.
• Cholesterol: 7 mg. • Sodium: 111 mg.
Exchanges: ½ vegetable, 1½ fruit, 3¼ fat

Mixed Mushroom Medley

¼ cup chopped shallots
2 tablespoons margarine or butter
3 tablespoons dry sherry
¼ teaspoon salt
¼ teaspoon freshly ground pepper
4 oz. crimini (brown) mushrooms, sliced (1½ cups)
4 oz. shiitake mushrooms, cut into quarters (1½ cups)
4 oz. oyster mushrooms, cut into ½-inch strips (1½ cups)

4 servings

In 2-cup measure, combine shallots and margarine. Microwave at High for 2½ to 3 minutes, or until shallots are tender, stirring once. Stir in sherry, salt and pepper.

In 2-quart casserole, combine mushrooms. Add shallot mixture. Toss to coat. Cover with wax paper or microwave cooking paper. Microwave at High for 3 to 4 minutes, or until oyster mushrooms are tender, stirring once. Drain. Serve with game meat, such as deer or duck, if desired.

Per Serving: Calories: 97 • Protein: 2 g.
• Carbohydrate: 7 g. • Fat: 6 g.
• Cholesterol: 0 • Sodium: 208 mg.
Exchanges: 1½ vegetable, 1¼ fat

Brussels Sprouts & Fennel ▲

1 lb. Brussels sprouts, trimmed
1 bulb fennel (8 to 10 oz.), thinly sliced
¼ cup water
¼ cup orange marmalade
⅛ teaspoon salt
⅛ teaspoon white pepper
2 teaspoons white vinegar
¾ teaspoon cornstarch
1 teaspoon snipped fresh fennel leaves

4 servings

Cut cross into stem of each sprout. In 2-quart casserole, combine sprouts, fennel bulb and water. Cover. Microwave at High for 12 to 15 minutes, or until sprouts are tender, stirring once. Drain. Cover to keep warm. Set aside.

In 1-cup measure, combine marmalade, salt and pepper. Microwave at High for 45 seconds to 1¼ minutes, or until mixture is hot and marmalade is melted.

In small bowl, combine vinegar and cornstarch. Stir into marmalade mixture. Microwave at High for 30 to 45 seconds, or until sauce is thickened and translucent, stirring every 30 seconds. Stir in fennel leaves. Spoon sauce over sprouts and fennel bulb.

Per Serving: Calories: 106 • Protein: 4 g. • Carbohydrate: 25 g. • Fat: 0
• Cholesterol: 0 • Sodium: 149 mg.
Exchanges: 2 vegetable, 1 fruit

Scallop, Black Bean & Avocado Salad ▲

1 lb. fresh bay scallops, rinsed and drained

Dressing:

⅓ cup lemon juice
¼ cup olive oil
¼ cup sliced green onions
2 tablespoons catsup
½ teaspoon ground cumin
½ teaspoon sugar
½ teaspoon seasoned salt
¼ teaspoon cayenne

2 medium tomatoes, seeded and chopped
   (2 cups)
1 can (15 oz.) black beans, rinsed and
   drained
1½ cups chopped green pepper
1 medium avocado, peeled and chopped
   (1 cup)

6 to 8 servings

In 9-inch round cake dish, arrange scallops in single layer. Set aside. In 2-cup measure, combine dressing ingredients. Drizzle 2 tablespoons dressing over scallops. Cover scallops with wax paper or microwave cooking paper. Microwave at 70% (Medium High) for 6 to 7 minutes, or until scallops are firm and opaque, stirring once to rearrange. Drain. Set aside.

In medium mixing bowl, combine remaining ingredients and remaining dressing. Add scallops. Toss to combine. Cover with plastic wrap. Chill.

Per Serving: Calories: 203 • Protein: 13 g. • Carbohydrate: 14 g.
• Fat: 11 g. • Cholesterol: 19 mg. • Sodium: 305 mg.
Exchanges: ¾ starch, 1¼ lean meat, ½ vegetable, 1½ fat

Sweet Potato Salad

3 medium sweet potatoes, peeled and
   cut into 2½ × ½-inch chunks (5 cups)
4¼ cups hot water, divided
2 cups broccoli flowerets
½ cup finely chopped fully cooked lean ham
⅓ cup sliced green onions

Dressing:

⅓ cup French dressing
⅓ cup sour cream
1 tablespoon snipped fresh chervil leaves

4 to 6 servings

In 2-quart casserole, combine potatoes and ¼ cup water. Cover. Microwave at High for 9 to 12 minutes, or just until potatoes are tender, stirring once. Drain. Set aside.

Place remaining 4 cups water in 8-cup measure. Cover with plastic wrap. Microwave at High for 10 to 12 minutes, or until boiling. Plunge broccoli into boiling water for 30 seconds, or until color brightens. Using slotted spoon, remove broccoli and immediately plunge into ice water. Drain.

In large mixing bowl or salad bowl, combine potatoes, broccoli, ham and onions. In small mixing bowl, combine dressing ingredients. Add to potato mixture. Toss to coat. Chill.

Per Serving: Calories: 230 • Protein: 6 g. • Carbohydrate: 31 g.
• Fat: 10 g. • Cholesterol: 13 mg. • Sodium: 400 mg.
Exchanges: 1½ starch, 1½ vegetable, 2 fat

◀ Succotash Escallop

- 2 ears corn on the cob (8 to 10 oz. each), kernels sliced off (1½ cups) and cobs discarded
- 1⅓ cups sliced green beans (1½-inch lengths)
- ½ cup chopped green pepper
- ½ cup sliced green onions
- ¼ cup water
- 1 large tomato, seeded and chopped (1½ cups)
- 2 tablespoons margarine or butter
- 2 tablespoons all-purpose flour
- ¼ teaspoon salt
- ⅛ to ¼ teaspoon freshly ground pepper
- 1 cup milk
- 1½ teaspoons Dijon mustard
- 2 tablespoons snipped fresh parsley

6 to 8 servings

In 2-quart casserole, combine corn, beans, green pepper, onions and water. Cover. Microwave at High for 9 to 11 minutes, or until beans are tender-crisp. Drain. Stir in tomato. Cover. Set aside.

In 2-cup measure, microwave margarine at High for 45 seconds to 1 minute, or until melted. Stir in flour, salt and pepper. Blend in milk and mustard. Microwave at High for 3 to 5 minutes, or until sauce is thickened, stirring after 2 minutes and then every minute. Stir in parsley.

Pour sauce over vegetable mixture. Toss to coat. Garnish with additional snipped fresh parsley, if desired.

Per Serving: Calories: 97 • Protein: 3 g.
• Carbohydrate: 13 g. • Fat: 4 g.
• Cholesterol: 4 mg. • Sodium: 155 mg.
Exchanges: ½ starch, ¾ vegetable, 1 fat

Asparagus with Capers

- 1½ lbs. asparagus spears, cut into 1½-inch lengths (4 cups)
- 4 oz. mushrooms, sliced (1 cup)
- 2 tablespoons water
- ¼ cup margarine or butter
- 1 to 2 tablespoons capers, rinsed and drained
- ¼ teaspoon freshly ground pepper

4 servings

In 2-quart casserole, combine asparagus, mushrooms and water. Cover. Microwave at High for 9 to 11 minutes, or until asparagus is tender-crisp, stirring once. Drain. Cover to keep warm. Set aside.

In 2-cup measure, microwave margarine at High for 1¼ to 1½ minutes, or until melted. Stir in capers and pepper. Add margarine mixture to asparagus and mushrooms. Toss to coat.

Per Serving: Calories: 129 • Protein: 3 g. • Carbohydrate: 5 g. • Fat: 12 g.
• Cholesterol: 0 • Sodium: 219 mg.
Exchanges: 1 vegetable, 2¼ fat

Tomatillo-sauced Salads

1 lb. tomatillos, husked, divided
1 cup chopped red onions
2 tablespoons olive oil
3 tablespoons snipped fresh cilantro
2 tablespoons lime juice
1 clove garlic, minced
1/4 teaspoon ground cumin
1/8 to 1/4 teaspoon crushed red pepper flakes
4 peeled mangos or medium tomatoes, sliced

6 to 8 servings

Coarsely chop enough tomatillos to make 1/3 cup. Set aside. Cut remaining tomatillos into quarters. In 2-quart casserole, combine quartered tomatillos, onions and oil. Cover. Microwave at High for 6 to 9 minutes, or until tomatillos are tender, stirring once.

In food processor or blender, combine tomatillo mixture and remaining ingredients, except mangos. Process until coarsely blended. Stir in reserved tomatillos. Chill. Arrange mango slices on lettuce-lined plates. Top evenly with tomatillo sauce.

Per Serving: Calories: 120 • Protein: 2 g. • Carbohydrate: 22 g.
• Fat: 4 g. • Cholesterol: 0 • Sodium: 5 mg.
Exchanges: 1½ vegetable, 1 fruit, ¾ fat

Honey-Dijon Broccoflower ▶

4 cups broccoflowerets
2 tablespoons water
1 cup red pepper strips
    (2 × 1/4-inch strips)
2 tablespoons honey
1 tablespoon plus 1 teaspoon
    Dijon mustard
1 teaspoon mustard seed
1 tablespoon snipped fresh
    chives

4 servings

In 2-quart casserole, combine broccoflower and water. Cover. Microwave at High for 7 to 9 minutes, or until tender. Drain. Stir in pepper strips. Cover to keep warm. Set aside.

In 1-cup measure, combine honey, mustard and mustard seed. Microwave at High for 30 to 45 seconds, or until mixture is hot and bubbly. Stir in chives. Pour mixture over vegetables. Toss to coat.

Per Serving: Calories: 73 • Protein: 2 g.
• Carbohydrate: 16 g. • Fat: 1 g.
• Cholesterol: 0 • Sodium: 166 mg.
Exchanges: 1¾ vegetable, ½ fruit

Sweet & Sour Glazed Onions

1¼ lbs. white pearl onions, peeled (4 cups)
  1 tablespoon plus 1 teaspoon margarine or butter
  2 tablespoons packed brown sugar
  1 teaspoon cornstarch
  ½ teaspoon dry mustard
  3 tablespoons catsup
  1 tablespoon plus 1 teaspoon cider vinegar
  1 tablespoon snipped watercress leaves

4 to 6 servings

In 2-quart casserole, combine onions and margarine. Cover. Microwave at High for 12 to 14 minutes, or until onions are tender, stirring once. Drain; reserve liquid. Cover onions to keep warm. Set aside.

In 1-cup measure, combine sugar, cornstarch and mustard. Blend in reserved liquid, the catsup and vinegar. Microwave at High for 1½ to 2 minutes, or until sauce is thickened and glossy, stirring every 30 seconds. Stir in watercress. Pour sauce over onions. Toss to coat. Serve with ham, if desired.

Per Serving: Calories: 82 • Protein: 1 g. • Carbohydrate: 15 g. • Fat: 3 g. • Cholesterol: 0 • Sodium: 129 mg.
Exchanges: 2 vegetable, ¼ fruit, ½ fat

Vegetable Shepherd's Pie ▲

Filling:
1½ cups red pepper strips (2 × ¼-inch strips)
  1 medium yellow squash, cut lengthwise into quarters, then crosswise into 1-inch lengths (1½ cups)
  1 cup sliced leek
  4 oz. crimini (brown) mushrooms, sliced (1½ cups)
  ½ cup thinly sliced peeled parsnip
  3 tablespoons water

  2 medium russet potatoes, peeled and cut into 1-inch cubes (2 cups)
  ½ cup water
  ¼ cup milk
  2 tablespoons margarine or butter
  2 tablespoons soy sauce
  ¼ teaspoon freshly ground pepper
  1 tablespoon plus 1 teaspoon cornstarch mixed with 2 tablespoons water
  1 tablespoon fresh thyme leaves
  1 tablespoon margarine or butter, melted
    Paprika

6 servings

Per Serving: Calories: 159 • Protein: 3 g. • Carbohydrate: 23 g. • Fat: 6 g. • Cholesterol: 1 mg. • Sodium: 427 mg.
Exchanges: ¾ starch, 2½ vegetable, 1¼ fat

How to Make Vegetable Shepherd's Pie

Heat conventional oven to 400°F. In 2-quart casserole, combine filling ingredients. Cover.

Microwave at High for 7 to 9 minutes, or until vegetables are tender-crisp, stirring once. Drain. Re-cover. Set filling aside.

Combine potatoes and ½ cup water in 1½-quart casserole. Cover.

Microwave at High for 13 to 15 minutes, or until tender, stirring once. Drain; reserve potato water. Add milk and 2 table-spoons margarine to potatoes.

Mash until smooth. Set aside. In 2-cup measure, combine reserved potato water plus enough water to make 1 cup, the soy sauce and pepper.

Microwave at High for 2½ to 3½ minutes, or until boiling. Stir in cornstarch mixture.

Microwave at High for 45 sec-onds to 1 minute, or until gravy is thickened and translucent, stirring every 30 seconds. Stir in thyme leaves. Set aside.

Spray 8-inch square baking dish with nonstick vegetable cooking spray. Spoon filling into prepared dish. Pour gravy over filling. Spread mashed potatoes evenly over all.

Brush potatoes with melted margarine. Sprinkle with paprika. Bake conventionally for 20 to 25 minutes, or until potatoes are golden brown. Let stand for 10 minutes before serving.

Spaghetti Squash au Gratin

1 spaghetti squash (about 2½ lbs.)
1 cup sliced leek
1 medium zucchini, sliced (1 cup)
1 tablespoon water
½ cup chopped red pepper
2 tablespoons all-purpose flour
¼ teaspoon salt
⅛ teaspoon white pepper
1 cup milk
½ cup shredded Swiss cheese
⅓ cup cornflake crumbs
1 tablespoon margarine or butter, melted

6 servings

Pierce squash deeply several times with sharp knife. Place on paper towel in oven. Microwave at High for 13 to 15 minutes, or until squash yields to pressure and feels soft, turning over once. Let stand for 5 minutes.

Cut squash in half crosswise. Scoop out and discard seeds and fibers. Twist out long strands of flesh with fork. Place in 10-inch square casserole. Set aside.

In 1½-quart casserole, combine leek, zucchini and water. Cover. Microwave at High for 4 to 6 minutes, or until zucchini is tender. Drain. Add zucchini mixture and red pepper to squash. Toss to combine. Cover. Set aside.

In 2-cup measure, combine flour, salt and white pepper. Blend in milk. Microwave at High for 3 to 4 minutes, or until mixture thickens and bubbles, stirring every minute. Stir in cheese until melted. Pour mixture over vegetables. Toss to coat.

In small mixing bowl, combine crumbs and margarine. Sprinkle crumb mixture evenly over vegetable mixture. Microwave at High for 4 to 5 minutes, or until hot and bubbly around edges, rotating casserole once.

Per Serving: Calories: 172 • Protein: 6 g. • Carbohydrate: 23 g. • Fat: 7 g.
• Cholesterol: 14 mg. • Sodium: 262 mg.
Exchanges: ½ starch, ¼ meat, 3 vegetable, 1 fat

Winter Squash Soufflé

- 1 acorn squash (1½ lbs.), peeled and cut into 1-inch cubes
- 3 tablespoons water
- 3 tablespoons plus 1 teaspoon butter or margarine, divided
- 2 egg yolks
- ¼ teaspoon salt
- ¼ teaspoon freshly ground pepper
- 1½ teaspoons snipped fresh rosemary leaves (optional)
- 1 tablespoon plus 1 teaspoon dried grated Parmesan cheese
- 3 egg whites
- ¼ teaspoon cream of tartar

4 to 6 servings

In 1½-quart casserole, combine squash and water. Cover. Microwave at High for 9 to 11 minutes, or until tender. Drain. In food processor or blender, combine squash, 3 tablespoons butter, the egg yolks, salt and pepper. Process until smooth. Pour into large mixing bowl. Stir in rosemary leaves. Set aside.

Using remaining 1 teaspoon butter, grease 2-quart soufflé dish. Sprinkle inside of dish with Parmesan cheese, tilting dish to coat sides. Set aside.

In medium mixing bowl, combine egg whites and cream of tartar. Beat at high speed of electric mixer until stiff but not dry. Stir scoop of egg whites into squash mixture. Add remaining egg whites to squash mixture and gently fold in. Pour mixture into prepared soufflé dish. Microwave at 30% (Medium Low) for 18 to 30 minutes, or until top is dry, rotating dish ¼ turn 3 or 4 times. Serve immediately.

NOTE: A fluffier soufflé is produced in a microwave with a carousel, since the final cooking stage will not be interrupted.

Per Serving: Calories: 124 • Protein: 4 g. • Carbohydrate: 9 g. • Fat: 8 g. • Cholesterol: 89 mg. • Sodium: 208 mg. Exchanges: ½ starch, ⅓ meat, 1¼ fat

Squash Medley ▲

- 1 lb. patty pan squash (1½ to 2 inches in diameter), halved
- 1 medium yellow squash, sliced (1 cup)
- ½ cup carrot strips (2 × ¼-inch strips)
- ¼ cup finely chopped onion
- 3 tablespoons water
- 3 tablespoons margarine or butter
- 1 tablespoon snipped fresh dill weed

4 servings

In 2-quart casserole, combine squashes, carrot strips, onion and water. Cover. Microwave at High for 10 to 13 minutes, or until patty pan squash are tender. Drain. Cover to keep warm. Let stand for 5 minutes.

In 1-cup measure, microwave margarine at High for 1 to 1¼ minutes, or until melted. Stir in dill weed. Add to squash mixture. Toss to coat.

Per Serving: Calories: 114 • Protein: 2 g. • Carbohydrate: 8 g. • Fat: 9 g. • Cholesterol: 0 • Sodium: 108 mg. Exchanges: 1½ vegetable, 1¾ fat

Cheesy Tomato Rice

1   cup uncooked long-grain white rice
1   teaspoon margarine or butter
1/2 teaspoon salt
2   cups hot water
1   large tomato, seeded and chopped
    (1 1/2 cups)
1/2 cup crumbled chèvre cheese (goat cheese)
1   tablespoon snipped fresh basil leaves
1/8 to 1/4 teaspoon freshly ground pepper

4 to 6 servings

In 2-quart casserole, combine rice, margarine
and salt. Stir in hot water. Cover. Microwave at
High for 5 minutes. Microwave at 50% (Medium)
for 12 to 18 minutes longer, or until rice is tender
and liquid is absorbed. Let stand, covered, for
5 minutes. Add remaining ingredients. Toss
to combine.

Variation: Substitute mozzarella cheese for chèvre.

Per Serving: Calories: 168 • Protein: 5 g. • Carbohydrate: 27 g.
• Fat: 4 g. • Cholesterol: 9 mg. • Sodium: 253 mg.
Exchanges: 1 1/4 starch, 1/2 high-fat meat, 1 vegetable

Sage Potatoes ▲

2   medium russet potatoes, thinly sliced,
    rinsed and drained
1/4 cup water
1/2 cup half-and-half
1   tablespoon snipped fresh sage leaves
1   clove garlic, minced
1/4 teaspoon salt
1/4 teaspoon freshly ground pepper
1 1/2 cups shredded Co-Jack cheese

4 to 6 servings

Spread potato slices in 10-inch square casserole. Sprinkle with water. Cover. Microwave at
High for 10 to 12 minutes, or until tender-crisp,
stirring once. Drain. Set aside.

In 2-cup measure, combine remaining ingredients, except cheese. Pour mixture over potatoes.
Sprinkle top evenly with cheese. Heat conventional broiler. Microwave potato mixture at High
for 6 to 8 minutes, or until potatoes are tender,
rotating dish once. Place casserole under broiler
with surface of food 5 inches from heat. Broil for
6 to 7 minutes, or until golden brown.

Per Serving: Calories: 198 • Protein: 9 g. • Carbohydrate: 15 g.
• Fat: 11 g. • Cholesterol: 34 mg. • Sodium: 264 mg.
Exchanges: 1 starch, 1 meat, 1 fat

Vegetable Stir-fry Primavera ▲

4 oz. uncooked spinach fettucini
1 medium red pepper, cut into 1-inch chunks
   (1⅓ cups)
½ cup sliced peeled carrot
1 tablespoon water
1 medium cucumber, peeled, cut lengthwise
   into quarters and sliced (2 cups)
3 tablespoons Italian dressing
1 tablespoon snipped fresh marjoram leaves

6 servings

Prepare fettucini as directed on package. Rinse with hot water. Drain. Place in large mixing bowl. Cover to keep warm. Set aside.

In 2-quart casserole, combine red pepper, carrot and water. Cover. Microwave at High for 4 to 6 minutes, or until vegetables are tender-crisp, stirring once. Drain.

Stir in remaining ingredients. Cover. Microwave at High for 1 to 2 minutes, or until hot. Add vegetable mixture to fettucini. Toss to combine.

Per Serving: Calories: 104 • Protein: 3 g. • Carbohydrate: 14 g.
• Fat: 4 g. • Cholesterol: 21 mg. • Sodium: 79 mg.
Exchanges: ½ starch, 1 vegetable, 1 fat

Jícama with Yogurt Sauce

1- lb. jícama, peeled and cut into
   2½ × ¼-inch strips
¼ cup water
½ cup plain nonfat or low-fat yogurt
1 tablespoon snipped fresh dill weed or
   chives
2 teaspoons lemon juice
1 teaspoon sugar
⅛ teaspoon garlic powder
⅛ teaspoon salt
   Dash white pepper

4 servings

In 2-quart casserole, combine jícama and water. Cover. Microwave at High for 6 to 7 minutes, or until hot, stirring once. (Jícama should remain tender-crisp.) Drain. Let stand, covered, for 5 minutes. In small bowl, combine remaining ingredients. Serve with jícama.

Per Serving: Calories: 64 • Protein: 3 g. • Carbohydrate: 13 g.
• Fat: 0 • Cholesterol: 1 mg. • Sodium: 98 mg.
Exchanges: 2 vegetable

Whole Wheat Squash Quiche

1 cup whole wheat flour
1/2 teaspoon salt
1/3 cup vegetable shortening
2 tablespoons margarine or
   butter, room temperature
2 to 3 tablespoons cold water
4 slices bacon
1 acorn squash (1 1/4 lbs.),
   peeled and cut into 1-inch
   cubes
3 tablespoons hot water
1 medium zucchini squash,
   sliced (1 cup)
1/2 cup finely chopped onion
2 tablespoons all-purpose
   flour
1/4 teaspoon freshly ground
   pepper
1/4 teaspoon ground nutmeg
1/3 cup milk
4 eggs

4 to 6 servings

In large mixing bowl, combine whole wheat flour, salt, shortening and margarine. Beat at low speed of electric mixer until particles resemble coarse crumbs. Sprinkle cold water, 1 tablespoon at a time, over flour mixture, mixing with fork until particles are moistened and cling together. Form dough into ball. Place on lightly floured surface.

Roll dough into 11-inch circle. Fit circle into 9-inch pie plate. Flute edges. Prick bottom of crust with fork at 1/2-inch intervals. Microwave at High for 6 to 8 minutes, or until dry, rotating 1/2 turn every 3 minutes. Set aside. Layer 3 paper towels on plate. Arrange bacon on paper towels. Cover with another paper towel. Microwave at High for 3 to 6 minutes, or until bacon is brown and crisp. Cool slightly. Crumble. Set aside.

In 2-quart casserole, combine acorn squash and hot water. Cover. Microwave at High for 5 minutes. Add zucchini and onion. Mix well. Re-cover. Microwave at High for 8 to 12 minutes, or until squashes are tender, stirring once. Drain. Set aside.

In medium mixing bowl, combine all-purpose flour, pepper and nutmeg. Blend in milk. Beat in eggs. Add egg mixture and bacon to squash mixture. Pour into prepared crust. Center pie plate on saucer in oven. Microwave at 70% (Medium High) for 9 to 12 minutes, or until center is set, rotating twice. Let stand for 5 minutes.

Per Serving: Calories: 332 • Protein: 10 g. • Carbohydrate: 27 g. • Fat: 21 g.
• Cholesterol: 147 mg. • Sodium: 347 mg.
Exchanges: 1 1/2 starch, 3/4 medium-fat meat, 1 vegetable, 3 1/4 fat

Chilied Stuffed Zucchini ▶

8 oz. lean ground beef,
   crumbled
½ cup chopped onion
1 clove garlic, minced
3 medium zucchini (6 oz.
   each)
2 Roma tomatoes, chopped
   (1 cup)
¼ cup tomato paste
1 teaspoon cumin seed
¼ to ½ teaspoon cayenne
½ cup shredded Cheddar
   cheese
¼ cup snipped fresh cilantro
   leaves
¼ cup unseasoned dry bread
   crumbs

6 servings

Per Serving: Calories: 162 • Protein: 11 g.
• Carbohydrate: 10 g. • Fat: 9 g.
• Cholesterol: 32 mg. • Sodium: 197 mg.
Exchanges: ¼ starch, 1¼ medium-fat
meat, 1 vegetable, ½ fat

How to Microwave Chilied Stuffed Zucchini

Combine beef, onion and garlic in 1½-quart casserole. Cover with wax paper or microwave cooking paper. Microwave at High for 3 to 4 minutes, or until meat is no longer pink, stirring once to break apart. Drain. Set aside.

Cut zucchini in half lengthwise. Scoop out pulp, leaving ¼-inch shells. Coarsely chop pulp. Set shells aside. Add pulp, tomatoes, paste, cumin and cayenne to beef mixture. Mix well.

Microwave at High for 4 to 6 minutes, or until mixture is hot and zucchini is tender, stirring once. Stir in remaining ingredients. Spoon mixture evenly into shells. Arrange stuffed zucchini on roasting rack.

Cover with wax paper or microwave cooking paper. Microwave at High for 8 to 13 minutes, or until zucchini is tender, rotating rack and re-arranging zucchini once. Serve with sour cream and additional shredded cheese, if desired.

Eggplant Pizza

1 small eggplant (8 oz.),
  thinly sliced
½ teaspoon salt
1 tablespoon yellow cornmeal
1 pkg. (10 oz.) refrigerated
  pizza crust dough
1 can (8 oz.) pizza sauce
4 oz. fresh mozzarella
  cheese, sliced
2 Roma tomatoes, thinly
  sliced
2 tablespoons snipped fresh
  oregano

4 to 6 servings

Sprinkle eggplant slices evenly with salt. Place slices in colander. Let stand for 30 minutes. Rinse and blot with paper towels to remove excess moisture. Arrange slices, slightly overlapping, in 10-inch square casserole. Microwave at High for 6 to 8 minutes, or until tender, rearranging and turning slices over once. Set aside.

Heat conventional oven to 425°F. Spray 12-inch pizza pan with nonstick vegetable cooking spray. Sprinkle evenly with cornmeal. Press dough into pan. Spread sauce on crust to within ½ inch of edge. Arrange cheese slices over sauce. Top evenly with eggplant, tomatoes and oregano. Bake for 13 to 15 minutes, or until crust is golden brown. Let stand for 5 minutes before serving. If desired, drizzle extra-virgin olive oil over pizza before serving.

Per Serving: Calories: 215 • Protein: 9 g.
• Carbohydrate: 29 g. • Fat: 7 g.
• Cholesterol: 13 mg. • Sodium: 497 mg.
Exchanges: 1½ starch, 1 medium-fat meat, 1½ vegetable

Buttered Sweet Pepper Ravioli ▲

4 oz. mushrooms, sliced
  (1 cup)
½ cup green pepper strips
  (2 × ¼-inch strips)
½ cup red pepper strips
  (2 × ¼-inch strips)
1 clove garlic, minced

3 tablespoons margarine or
  butter
1 tablespoon snipped fresh
  oregano, basil or thyme
  leaves
1 pkg. (9 oz.) uncooked fresh
  cheese ravioli

3 to 4 servings

In 2-quart casserole, combine mushrooms, peppers and garlic. Cover. Microwave at High for 3 to 4 minutes, or just until mushrooms are tender, stirring once. Drain. Add margarine. Microwave at High, uncovered, for 1 to 2 minutes, or until margarine is melted, stirring once. Add oregano. Stir to combine.

Meanwhile, prepare ravioli as directed on package. Drain. Place ravioli in large mixing bowl or serving bowl. Add pepper mixture. Toss to combine. Serve with shredded fresh Parmesan cheese, if desired.

Per Serving: Calories: 293 • Protein: 11 g. • Carbohydrate: 25 g. • Fat: 17 g.
• Cholesterol: 56 mg. • Sodium: 372 mg.
Exchanges: 1½ starch, ¾ medium-fat meat, ½ vegetable, 2½ fat

Seafood Salsa Pitas

1 small onion, thinly sliced
1 medium green pepper,
    cut into 1-inch chunks
    (1⅓ cups)
2 teaspoons vegetable oil
1 clove garlic, minced
½ teaspoon ground cumin
¼ teaspoon salt
¼ teaspoon freshly ground
    pepper
3½ oz. fresh shiitake
    mushrooms, cut into
    quarters (2 cups)
2 ears corn on the cob (8 to
    10 oz. each), kernels
    sliced off (1½ cups) and
    cobs discarded
8 oz. imitation crab meat,
    shredded
4 pita loaves (6-inch), cut in
    half
    Lettuce leaves

6 to 8 servings

In 1½-quart casserole, combine onion, green pepper, oil, garlic, cumin, salt and pepper. Cover. Microwave at High for 3 to 5 minutes, or until onion is tender-crisp, stirring once. Cover to keep warm. Set aside.

In 2-quart casserole, combine mushrooms and corn. Cover. Microwave at High for 5 to 8 minutes, or until mushrooms are tender and corn is hot, stirring once.

Add onion mixture and crab meat to corn mixture. Toss to combine. Line pita halves with lettuce leaves. Spoon corn mixture evenly into pitas. Garnish with chopped tomato, if desired.

Per Serving: Calories: 152 • Protein: 7 g.
• Carbohydrate: 28 g. • Fat: 2 g.
• Cholesterol: 4 mg. • Sodium: 497 mg.
Exchanges: 1½ starch, ½ lean meat,
½ vegetable

Mango-Shrimp Curry ▲

2 tablespoons margarine or
    butter
½ cup chopped onion
½ medium green pepper, cut
    into 1-inch chunks (⅔ cup)
1 clove garlic, minced
1 tablespoon all-purpose flour
1 tablespoon curry powder

½ cup coconut milk
12 oz. fresh medium shrimp,
    shelled and deveined
½ cup chopped peeled
    mango
    Hot cooked rice

4 servings

In 2-quart casserole, microwave margarine at High for 45 seconds to 1 minute, or until melted. Add onion, green pepper and garlic. Stir to combine. Cover. Microwave at High for 3 to 4 minutes, or until pepper is tender-crisp, stirring once. Stir in flour and curry powder. Blend in coconut milk. Add shrimp. Toss to coat. Cover. Microwave at 70% (Medium High) for 7 to 9 minutes, or until shrimp are firm and opaque, stirring twice. Stir in mango. Serve over rice. Garnish with toasted coconut flakes, if desired.

Per Serving: Calories: 217 • Protein: 15 g. • Carbohydrate: 10 g. • Fat: 13 g.
• Cholesterol: 105 mg. • Sodium: 175 mg.
Exchanges: 2 lean meat, ½ vegetable, ½ fruit, 1½ fat

Salmon Steaks with Cucumber Hollandaise

4 salmon steaks (8 oz. each), 1 inch thick

Marinade:

½ cup vegetable oil
¼ cup rice wine vinegar or white wine vinegar
 1 teaspoon grated lemon peel
 1 tablespoon lemon juice
 1 teaspoon snipped fresh fennel leaves
 1 teaspoon sugar
¼ teaspoon salt
¼ teaspoon freshly ground pepper

 1 pkg. (1.25 oz.) hollandaise sauce mix
½ cup water
 1 tablespoon vegetable oil
⅓ cup finely chopped peeled seeded
       cucumber
 1 teaspoon snipped fresh fennel leaves

4 servings

Place steaks in shallow dish. Set aside. In small mixing bowl, combine marinade ingredients. Pour marinade over steaks, turning to coat. Cover with plastic wrap. Chill 1 to 2 hours, turning steaks over occasionally.

Place sauce mix in 4-cup measure. Blend in water and oil. Microwave at High for 2½ to 3½ minutes, or until mixture thickens and bubbles, stirring every minute. Stir in cucumber and fennel. Cover sauce to keep warm. Set aside.

Drain and discard marinade from steaks. Arrange steaks on roasting rack with thickest portions toward outside. Cover with wax paper or micro-wave cooking paper. Microwave at 70% (Medium High) for 9 to 11 minutes, or until fish is firm and opaque and just begins to flake, rotating rack every 3 minutes. Let stand, covered, for 5 minutes. Serve steaks with sauce.

Per Serving: Calories: 475 • Protein: 42 g. • Carbohydrate: 5 g.
• Fat: 31 g. • Cholesterol: 157 mg. • Sodium: 476 mg.
Exchanges: ⅓ starch, 5½ lean meat, 3 fat

Swordfish Steaks with ▶ Avocado Salsa

Salsa:

- 1 medium avocado, peeled and finely chopped (1 cup)
- 2 tablespoons finely chopped red onion
- 1 tablespoon olive oil
- 1 tablespoon lime juice
- 2 teaspoons snipped fresh cilantro leaves
- 1/8 teaspoon salt

- 4 swordfish steaks (8 oz. each), 1 inch thick
- 2 teaspoons olive oil
- 1/8 to 1/4 teaspoon freshly ground pepper
- 1/8 teaspoon salt

4 servings

In small mixing bowl, combine salsa ingredients. Cover with plastic wrap. Chill 2 hours.

Arrange steaks on roasting rack with thickest portions toward outside. Brush steaks evenly with oil. Sprinkle evenly with pepper and salt. Cover with wax paper or microwave cooking paper.

Microwave at 70% (Medium High) for 9 to 11 minutes, or until fish is firm and opaque and just begins to flake, rotating rack every 3 minutes. Let stand, covered, for 5 minutes. Serve steaks with salsa.

Per Serving: Calories: 378 • Protein: 41 g.
• Carbohydrate: 4 g. • Fat: 21 g.
• Cholesterol: 79 mg. • Sodium: 326 mg.
Exchanges: 1/3 starch, 5 1/2 lean meat, 1 fat

Rosemary Trout

- 4 whole drawn rainbow trout (6 to 8 oz. each)
- 1/4 teaspoon salt
- 1/4 teaspoon freshly ground pepper
- 4 sprigs fresh rosemary
- 1 tablespoon olive oil

4 servings

Sprinkle cavities of trout evenly with salt and pepper. Place 1 sprig rosemary in each cavity. Arrange trout in 10-inch square casserole. Brush evenly with oil. Cover.

Microwave at High for 8 to 10 minutes, or until fish begins to flake when fork is inserted at backbone in thickest part of fish, rotating casserole and turning fish over once. Let stand, covered, for 5 minutes.

Per Serving: Calories: 113 • Protein: 14 g. • Carbohydrate: 0 • Fat: 6 g.
• Cholesterol: 39 mg. • Sodium: 154 mg.
Exchanges: 2 lean meat

Clam Mushroom Pizza ▲

1 tablespoon margarine or butter
2 tablespoons all-purpose flour
1/4 teaspoon salt
1/8 teaspoon white pepper
1/3 cup dry white wine
1 can (6 1/2 oz.) minced clams, drained (reserve
   1/3 cup juice)
1/4 cup snipped fresh parsley
2 tablespoons snipped fresh oregano leaves
1 tablespoon yellow cornmeal
1 pkg. (10 oz.) refrigerated pizza crust dough
2 oz. fresh shiitake mushrooms, sliced (3/4 cup)
2 oz. fresh oyster mushrooms, sliced (3/4 cup)
1/4 cup red pepper strips (1 1/2 × 1/8-inch strips)
1 cup shredded mozzarella cheese (optional)

4 to 6 servings

Heat conventional oven to 425°F. In 4-cup measure, microwave margarine at High for 45 seconds to 1 minute, or until melted. Stir in flour, salt and white pepper. Blend in wine and reserved clam juice. Microwave at High for 2 to 3 minutes, or until mixture thickens and bubbles, stirring every minute. Stir in parsley and oregano. Set sauce aside.

Spray 12-inch pizza pan with nonstick vegetable cooking spray. Sprinkle evenly with cornmeal. Press dough into pan. Spread sauce on crust to within 1/2 inch of edge. Top evenly with clams, mushrooms and red pepper. Sprinkle cheese evenly over pizza. Bake conventionally for 13 to 15 minutes, or until crust is golden brown. Let stand for 5 minutes before serving.

Per Serving: Calories: 192 • Protein: 9 g. • Carbohydrate: 27 g.
• Fat: 4 g. • Cholesterol: 11 mg. • Sodium: 365 mg.
Exchanges: 1 3/4 starch, 1 lean meat, 1/4 vegetable

Spinach & Shrimp Pizza

1 tablespoon margarine or
   butter
2 tablespoons all-purpose
   flour
1/4 teaspoon salt
1/4 teaspoon freshly ground
   pepper
2/3 cup milk
2 tablespoons shredded
   fresh Parmesan cheese
1 tablespoon snipped fresh
   oregano leaves
12 oz. fresh medium shrimp,
   shelled and deveined
1 tablespoon lemon juice
1 tablespoon olive oil
1 clove garlic, minced
8 cups torn spinach leaves
1 tablespoon yellow cornmeal
1 pkg. (10 oz.) refrigerated
   pizza crust dough
3/4 cup shredded Cheddar
   cheese

4 to 6 servings

Heat conventional oven to 425°F. In 4-cup measure, microwave margarine at High for 45 seconds to 1 minute, or until melted. Stir in flour, salt and pepper. Blend in milk. Microwave at High for 3 to 3 1/2 minutes, or until mixture thickens and bubbles, stirring every minute. Add Parmesan cheese and oregano. Stir until cheese is melted. Set sauce aside.

In 3-quart casserole, combine shrimp, juice, oil and garlic. Cover. Microwave at 70% (Medium High) for 4 to 6 minutes, or until shrimp are firm and opaque, stirring once. Add spinach. Re-cover. Microwave at High for 1 1/2 to 2 minutes, or just until spinach is wilted, stirring once. Drain. Set aside.

Spray 12-inch pizza pan with nonstick vegetable cooking spray. Sprinkle evenly with cornmeal. Press dough into pan. Spread sauce on crust to within 1/2 inch of edge. Top evenly with shrimp mixture and Cheddar cheese. Bake conventionally for 13 to 15 minutes, or until crust is golden brown. Let stand for 5 minutes before serving.

Per Serving: Calories: 321 • Protein: 21 g. • Carbohydrate: 30 g. • Fat: 13 g.
• Cholesterol: 90 mg. • Sodium: 611 mg.
Exchanges: 1 3/4 starch, 2 lean meat, 3/4 vegetable, 1 1/2 fat

Orange Roughy with Papaya Sauce

Sauce:
1 medium papaya, peeled, seeded and chopped
1 tablespoon sugar
1 tablespoon lemon juice
1/2 teaspoon grated fresh gingerroot

1 lb. orange roughy fillets, 1/2 inch thick, cut into serving-size pieces
2 tablespoons white wine Worcestershire sauce
1 medium avocado, peeled and sliced

4 servings

Per Serving: Calories: 271 • Protein: 18 g. • Carbohydrate: 16 g. • Fat: 16 g. • Cholesterol: 23 mg. • Sodium: 143 mg. Exchanges: 2 1/2 lean meat, 1 fruit, 1 1/2 fat

How to Microwave Orange Roughy with Papaya Sauce

Place sauce ingredients in food processor or blender. Process until smooth. Pour into 4-cup measure. Microwave at High for 3 to 4 minutes, or until hot, stirring once. Cover sauce to keep warm. Set aside.

Arrange fillets in 10-inch square casserole with thickest portions toward outside. Brush both sides evenly with Worcestershire sauce. Cover.

Microwave at 70% (Medium High) for 6 to 8 minutes, or until fish is firm and opaque and just begins to flake, rearranging fillets once. Let stand, covered, for 3 minutes. Arrange fillets on serving plates. Spoon sauce evenly over fillets. Top with avocado slices.

Triple Macaroni & Cheese ▶

- 12 oz. uncooked rainbow rotini (4 cups)
- 3 tablespoons margarine or butter
- 3 tablespoons all-purpose flour
- 1/4 teaspoon freshly ground pepper
- 1 1/2 cups milk
- 1 cup shredded hard farmer cheese
- 1/2 cup crumbled Gorgonzola cheese
- 1 medium tomato, seeded and coarsely chopped (1 cup)
- 1/4 cup slivered almonds (optional)
- 2 tablespoons snipped fresh chives
- 1 tablespoon fresh thyme leaves
- 2 oz. fresh Romano cheese, sliced into thin strips

6 to 8 servings

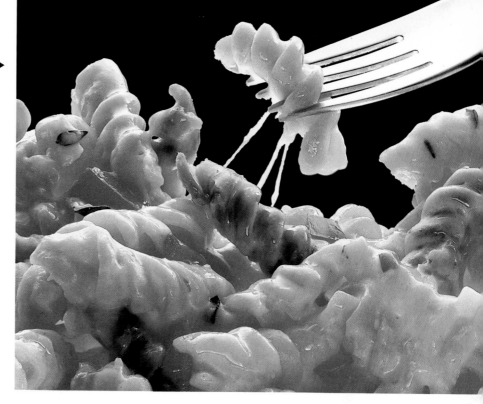

Prepare rotini as directed on package. Rinse and drain. Place in 3-quart casserole. Cover to keep warm. Set aside.

In 4-cup measure, microwave margarine at High for 1 to 1 1/4 minutes, or until melted. Stir in flour and pepper. Blend in milk. Microwave at High for 4 1/2 to 6 minutes, or until mixture thickens and bubbles, stirring every minute. Add farmer and Gorgonzola cheeses to mixture. Stir until cheeses are melted.

Add cheese mixture, tomato, almonds, chives and thyme to rotini. Toss to combine. Microwave at High for 3 minutes. Stir. Arrange Romano slices evenly over top. Microwave at High for 2 to 3 minutes, or until Romano is melted, rotating casserole once.

Per Serving: Calories: 335 • Protein: 16 g.
• Carbohydrate: 39 g. • Fat: 14 g.
• Cholesterol: 30 mg. • Sodium: 385 mg.
Exchanges: 2 1/4 starch, 1 high-fat meat, 1 fat

Florentine Sole Soufflé

- 2 tablespoons dried grated Parmesan cheese
- 8 cups torn spinach leaves
- 1/3 cup shredded radishes
- 1/3 cup shredded carrot
- 3 tablespoons all-purpose flour
- 1/4 teaspoon salt
- 1/4 teaspoon freshly ground pepper
- 1 cup milk
- 1 cup shredded hard farmer cheese
- 2 egg yolks, beaten
- 12 oz. sole fillets, 1/2 inch thick, cut into 1-inch cubes
- 5 egg whites

4 servings

Heat conventional oven to 350°F. Spray 2-quart soufflé dish with nonstick vegetable cooking spray. Sprinkle inside of dish with Parmesan cheese, tilting dish to coat sides. Set aside. Place spinach in 3-quart casserole. Cover. Microwave at High for 1 to 3 minutes, or just until wilted, stirring once. Add radishes and carrot. Mix well. Set aside.

In 4-cup measure, combine flour, salt and pepper. Blend in milk. Microwave at High for 3 1/2 to 4 1/2 minutes, or until mixture thickens and bubbles, stirring every minute. Add farmer cheese. Stir until cheese is melted. Place egg yolks in small mixing bowl. Stir small amount of hot cheese mixture gradually into egg yolks. Blend egg yolks back into cheese mixture. Add cheese mixture and sole to spinach mixture. Mix well. Set aside.

Place egg whites in large mixing bowl. Beat at high speed of electric mixer until stiff but not dry. Fold into spinach mixture. Pour mixture into prepared soufflé dish. Bake conventionally for 45 to 50 minutes, or until soufflé is golden brown and knife inserted in center comes out clean. Serve immediately.

Per Serving: Calories: 310 • Protein: 37 g. • Carbohydrate: 15 g. • Fat: 13 g.
• Cholesterol: 178 mg. • Sodium: 625 mg.
Exchanges: 1/4 starch, 4 1/2 lean meat, 1 1/2 vegetable, 1/4 low-fat milk

Citrus-glazed Chicken

3 - lb. whole broiler-fryer
   chicken
¼ teaspoon seasoned salt
¼ teaspoon freshly ground
   pepper
1 small cooking apple, cored
   and cut into ½-inch cubes
1 medium red pear, cored
   and cut into ½-inch cubes
1 tablespoon snipped fresh
   Italian parsley leaves
1 tablespoon snipped fresh
   dill weed
1 tablespoon snipped sorrel
   leaves, stems removed
1 tablespoon sherry vinegar

Glaze:
½ cup orange juice
1 tablespoon sherry vinegar
2 teaspoons cornstarch

4 to 6 servings

Per Serving: Calories: 280 • Protein: 28 g.
• Carbohydrate: 10 g. • Fat: 14 g.
• Cholesterol: 88 mg. • Sodium: 133 mg.
Exchanges: 4 lean meat, ⅔ fruit, ¼ fat

How to Microwave Citrus-glazed Chicken

Rub outside of chicken evenly with salt and pepper. In medium mixing bowl, combine apple, pear, parsley, dill, sorrel and vinegar.

Spoon apple mixture into cavity of chicken. Secure legs together with string. Place chicken breast-side-up on roasting rack.

Microwave at High for 21 to 33 minutes, or until internal temperature in thickest portions of both thighs registers 185°F and internal temperature of stuffing registers 150°F, rotating rack twice. Let stand for 10 minutes before carving. Meanwhile, in 2-cup measure, combine glaze ingredients. Microwave at High for 2 to 3 minutes, or until glaze is thickened and translucent, stirring every minute. Spoon over chicken.

Turkey Pot Roast*

- 2 turkey tenderloins (8 to 10 oz. each)
- 2 sprigs fresh rosemary
- 1/4 teaspoon seasoned salt
- 1/4 teaspoon freshly ground pepper
- 4 small red potatoes, thinly sliced, rinsed and drained
- 1 1/2 cups sliced green beans (1 1/2-inch lengths)
- 1 cup peeled white pearl onions
- 1/2 cup red pepper strips (2 × 1/4-inch strips)
- 1 pkg. (0.87 oz.) brown gravy mix
- 3/4 cup water
- 1/4 cup dry white wine

4 to 5 servings

Cut lengthwise slit in each tenderloin to within 1 inch of opposite side to form pocket. Place 1 sprig rosemary in each pocket. Sprinkle outside of tenderloins evenly with salt and pepper.

Place tenderloins in center of 10-inch square casserole. Arrange potatoes, beans, onions and red pepper around tenderloins. Set aside. Place gravy mix in 2-cup measure. Blend in water and wine. Pour mixture over vegetables. Cover with wax paper or microwave cooking paper.

Microwave at High for 18 to 21 minutes, or until turkey is firm and no longer pink, stirring vegetables and rotating casserole 2 or 3 times. Let stand, covered, for 5 minutes. Remove rosemary from tenderloins before serving.

* Recipe not recommended for ovens with less than 600 cooking watts.

Per Serving: Calories: 244 • Protein: 31 g. • Carbohydrate: 26 g. • Fat: 1 g.
• Cholesterol: 71 mg. • Sodium: 370 mg.
Exchanges: 1 1/4 starch, 3 lean meat, 1 1/2 vegetable

Turkey Tomato Meatloaf ▲

- 1 lb. ground turkey, crumbled
- 2 Roma tomatoes, chopped (1 cup)
- 1/2 cup unseasoned dry bread crumbs
- 1 egg
- 1/4 cup snipped arugula, stems removed
- 1 tablespoon fresh thyme leaves
- 1/2 teaspoon salt
- 1/4 teaspoon freshly ground pepper

6 servings

In medium mixing bowl, combine all ingredients. Shape mixture into loaf. Place into 8 × 4-inch loaf dish. Microwave at High for 13 to 15 minutes, or until meatloaf is firm and internal temperature registers 150°F in center, rotating twice. Let stand, covered, with foil, for 5 minutes.

Per Serving: Calories: 160 • Protein: 16 g.
• Carbohydrate: 8 g. • Fat: 7 g.
• Cholesterol: 91 mg. • Sodium: 329 mg.
Exchanges: 1/2 starch, 2 lean meat, 1/4 vegetable

Cumberland Chicken Toss

   1 tablespoon vegetable oil
  ¼ teaspoon seasoned salt
  ¼ teaspoon freshly ground pepper
   2 boneless whole chicken breasts (8 to 10 oz.
       each), split in half, skin removed, cut into
       ½-inch strips
  ½ cup red currant jelly
   1 teaspoon grated lemon peel
  ¼ cup lemon juice
   2 tablespoons port wine
   1 tablespoon packed brown sugar
1½ teaspoons grated orange peel
   1 teaspoon Dijon mustard
   1 tablespoon cornstarch mixed with
       1 tablespoon water
   1 tablespoon snipped fresh chervil leaves

4 servings

In medium mixing bowl, combine oil, salt and pepper. Add chicken. Stir to coat. Heat 12-inch nonstick skillet conventionally over medium-high heat. Add chicken. Cook for 4 to 6 minutes, or until brown on both sides. Remove from heat. Set aside.

In 4-cup measure, combine jelly, lemon peel, juice, port, sugar, orange peel and mustard. Microwave at High for 3 to 4 minutes, or just until mixture boils, stirring once. Blend in cornstarch mixture. Microwave at High for 1 to 1½ minutes, or until sauce is thickened and translucent, stirring every minute. Stir in chervil.

In medium mixing bowl, combine sauce and chicken. Toss to coat. Serve over hot cooked noodles or rice, if desired. Garnish with sliced peeled kiwifruit and additional chervil, if desired.

Per Serving: Calories: 307 • Protein: 26 g. • Carbohydrate: 34 g.
• Fat: 7 g. • Cholesterol: 70 mg. • Sodium: 185 mg.
Exchanges: 3 lean meat, 2¼ fruit

Asparagus-stuffed Chicken Breast

3 boneless whole chicken breasts (8 to 10 oz. each), skin removed, split in half
12 oz. asparagus spears, trimmed to 6-inch lengths
1 tablespoon water
¼ cup snipped watercress leaves
1 tablespoon grated lemon peel
¼ teaspoon seasoned salt
¼ teaspoon freshly ground pepper
¼ cup margarine or butter
1 pkg. (0.9 oz.) béarnaise sauce mix
1 cup milk

6 servings

Place chicken between 2 sheets of plastic wrap. Gently pound to ¼-inch thickness with flat side of meat mallet. Set aside.

Arrange asparagus in 8-inch square baking dish. Sprinkle with water. Cover with plastic wrap. Microwave at High for 3 to 5 minutes, or until color brightens, rotating dish once.

Arrange asparagus evenly crosswise on center of each breast half. Sprinkle watercress and peel evenly over asparagus. Fold ends of chicken around asparagus and secure each bundle with wooden pick. Sprinkle with salt and pepper.

Arrange bundles seam-side-down on roasting rack with asparagus tips toward center. Cover with wax paper or microwave cooking paper. Microwave at 70% (Medium High) for 8 to 12 minutes, or until chicken is firm and no longer pink, rotating rack twice. Let stand for 5 minutes.

In 4-cup measure, microwave margarine at High for 1¼ to 1½ minutes, or until melted. Stir in sauce mix. Blend in milk. Microwave at High for 4 to 5 minutes, or until sauce thickens and bubbles, stirring every minute. Remove wooden picks from bundles. Spoon sauce over chicken.

Per Serving: Calories: 214 • Protein: 20 g. • Carbohydrate: 7 g. • Fat: 12 g.
• Cholesterol: 53 mg. • Sodium: 416 mg.
Exchanges: ¼ starch, 2¼ lean meat, ½ vegetable, 1¼ fat

Hearty Hamburger Stir-fry

  1 lb. lean ground beef,
      crumbled
 ½ teaspoon celery seed
  2 cups broccoli flowerets
  2 cups cauliflowerets
  2 small onions, cut into thin
      wedges
  1 cup red pepper strips
      (3 × ¼-inch strips)
  1 tablespoon plus
      1 teaspoon cornstarch
1½ teaspoons sugar
 ½ cup low-sodium soy sauce
  2 tablespoons dry sherry

                 4 to 6 servings

In 2-quart casserole, combine beef and celery seed. Cover with wax paper or microwave cooking paper. Microwave at High for 5 to 6 minutes, or until meat is no longer pink, stirring once to break apart. Drain. Set aside.

In 3-quart casserole, combine broccoli, cauliflower, onions and red pepper. Set aside.

In small mixing bowl, combine cornstarch and sugar. Blend in soy sauce and sherry. Add soy sauce mixture to vegetables. Mix well.

Microwave at High, uncovered, for 12 to 17 minutes, or until sauce is thickened and translucent, stirring twice. Stir in beef. Serve over hot cooked Ramen noodles or rice, if desired.

Per Serving: Calories: 207 • Protein: 17 g. • Carbohydrate: 12 g. • Fat: 11 g.
• Cholesterol: 44 mg. • Sodium: 848 mg.
Exchanges: 2 medium-fat meat, 2¼ vegetable

Wine-sauced Steak ▶

4 beef eye round steaks
    (4 oz. each), ¾ inch thick
¼ teaspoon salt
¼ teaspoon freshly ground
    pepper
½ cup thinly sliced carrot
¼ cup chopped shallots
2 teaspoons olive oil
2 tablespoons snipped fresh
    basil leaves
2 teaspoons cornstarch
½ teaspoon sugar
½ cup dry red wine
4 oz. mushrooms, sliced
    (1 cup)

4 servings

Sprinkle both sides of steaks evenly with salt and pepper. Set aside. In 4-cup measure, combine carrot, shallots and oil. Microwave at High for 4 to 6 minutes, or until carrot is tender-crisp. Set aside.

In 1-cup measure, combine basil, cornstarch and sugar. Blend in wine. Stir wine mixture into carrot mixture. Microwave at High for 1 to 1½ minutes, or until sauce is thickened and translucent, stirring every minute.

Stir in mushrooms. Microwave at High for 2 to 3 minutes, or until mushrooms are tender, stirring once. Cover with plastic wrap to keep warm. Set aside.

Spray 10-inch nonstick skillet with nonstick vegetable cooking spray. Heat skillet conventionally over medium-high heat. Cook steaks for 4 to 5 minutes, or until desired doneness, turning over once. Spoon sauce over steaks.

Per Serving: Calories: 222 • Protein: 26 g.
• Carbohydrate: 7 g. • Fat: 8 g.
• Cholesterol: 61 mg. • Sodium: 204 mg.
Exchanges: 3 lean meat, ¾ vegetable,
¼ fruit

Brussels Sprouts Meatloaf

8 oz. Brussels sprouts,
    trimmed, chopped
    (2 cups)
½ cup finely chopped red
    onion
1 clove garlic, minced
1 tablespoon vegetable oil
1 lb. lean ground beef,
    crumbled
⅓ cup unseasoned dry bread
    crumbs

1 egg
3 tablespoons snipped fresh
    basil leaves
1 tablespoon fresh thyme
    leaves
½ teaspoon seasoned salt
¼ to ½ teaspoon freshly
    ground pepper
2 medium russet potatoes,
    peeled and shredded
    (1½ cups)

6 servings

In 2-quart casserole, combine sprouts, onion, garlic and oil. Cover. Microwave at High for 6 to 8 minutes, or until onion is tender, stirring once. Set aside.

In large mixing bowl, combine remaining ingredients, except potatoes. Add potatoes and sprout mixture. Mix well.

Shape mixture into loaf. Place into 8 × 4-inch loaf dish. Microwave at High for 13 to 15 minutes, or until meatloaf is firm and internal temperature registers 150°F in center, rotating twice. Let stand, covered with foil, for 5 minutes.

Per Serving: Calories: 307 • Protein: 17 g. • Carbohydrate: 16 g. • Fat: 19 g.
• Cholesterol: 92 mg. • Sodium: 218 mg.
Exchanges: ¾ starch, 2 medium-fat meat, 1 vegetable, 2 fat

Italian Veggie Burgers

- 1 lb. lean ground beef, crumbled
- ½ cup shredded yellow squash
- ¼ cup chopped shallots
- ¼ cup snipped fresh basil leaves
- ¼ cup shredded fresh Parmesan cheese
- 1 tablespoon unseasoned dry bread crumbs
- ¼ teaspoon garlic powder
- ¼ teaspoon salt (optional)
- ¼ teaspoon freshly ground pepper

4 servings

In medium mixing bowl, combine all ingredients. Shape mixture into four 4-inch patties. Arrange patties on roasting rack. Cover with wax paper or microwave cooking paper.

Microwave at High for 6 to 8 minutes, or until patties are firm and meat is no longer pink, turning patties over and rotating rack once. Serve in lettuce-lined whole wheat buns with tomato slices, if desired.

Variation: Substitute ground chicken or turkey for ground beef.

Per Serving: Calories: 273 • Protein: 23 g. • Carbohydrate: 5 g.
• Fat: 17 g. • Cholesterol: 70 mg. • Sodium: 174 mg.
Exchanges: 3¼ medium-fat meat, 1 vegetable

Bistro Veal ▲

- 1- lb. boneless veal shoulder roast, cut into 1-inch cubes
- 1 cup coarsely chopped onions
- ½ teaspoon freshly ground pepper
- ¼ teaspoon salt
- 2 medium tomatoes, peeled and chopped (2 cups)
- 1 cup diagonally sliced carrots
- ¾ cup shelled peas (1 lb. unshelled)
- ½ cup dry white wine
- 1 tablespoon fresh thyme leaves
- 1 teaspoon dried oregano leaves
- 1 teaspoon dried summer savory leaves
- 2 tablespoons cornstarch mixed with 2 tablespoons water

4 servings

Per Serving: Calories: 236 • Protein: 26 g. • Carbohydrate: 19 g.
• Fat: 4 g. • Cholesterol: 98 mg. • Sodium: 262 mg.
Exchanges: 3 lean meat, 2 vegetable, ½ fruit

Spray 12-inch nonstick skillet with nonstick vegetable cooking spray. Heat skillet conventionally over medium-high heat. Add veal. Cook for 4 to 5 minutes, or just until meat is no longer pink, stirring occasionally.

Place veal in 3-quart casserole. Add onions, pepper and salt. Cover. Microwave at High for 4 to 6 minutes, or until onion is tender, stirring once.

Stir in remaining ingredients, except cornstarch mixture. Re-cover. Microwave at High for 4 to 6 minutes, or until carrots are tender-crisp, stirring once. Reduce power to 50% (Medium). Microwave for 20 to 25 minutes longer, or until carrots and meat are tender, stirring once or twice.

Stir in cornstarch mixture. Microwave at High for 30 seconds to 1 minute, or until liquid is thickened and translucent, stirring once. Serve over hot cooked noodles, if desired.

Oregano Beef Couscous

2¼ cups hot water
3 tablespoons plus 2 teaspoons olive oil, divided
½ teaspoon salt, divided
1½ cups uncooked couscous
1 cup halved cherry tomatoes
½ cup diagonally sliced green onions (1-inch lengths)
¼ cup snipped fresh oregano leaves
1 tablespoon chopped seeded jalapeño pepper
1 clove garlic, minced
¼ teaspoon freshly ground pepper
1½-lb. boneless beef round tip roast, cut into 2 × ½ × ¼-inch strips

6 servings

In 10-inch square casserole, combine water, 3 tablespoons oil and ¼ teaspoon salt. Cover. Microwave at High for 6 to 8 minutes, or until boiling. Stir in couscous, tomatoes, onions, oregano and jalapeño pepper. Re-cover. Let stand for 4 to 5 minutes, or until liquid is absorbed.

Meanwhile, in medium mixing bowl, combine remaining 2 teaspoons oil and ¼ teaspoon salt, the garlic and pepper. Add beef. Stir to coat.

Heat 12-inch nonstick skillet conventionally over medium-high heat. Add beef. Cook for 4 to 6 minutes, or just until meat is only slightly pink, stirring frequently. Using slotted spoon, add beef to casserole. Mix well.

Per Serving: Calories: 466 • Protein: 39 g. • Carbohydrate: 38 g. • Fat: 17 g. • Cholesterol: 92 mg. • Sodium: 264 mg. Exchanges: 2¼ starch, 4 lean meat, 1 vegetable, 1 fat

Veal Piccata ▲

3 tablespoons all-purpose flour
¼ teaspoon seasoned salt
¼ teaspoon freshly ground pepper
6 veal leg cutlets (4 oz. each), ¼ inch thick
1 tablespoon margarine or butter
1 tablespoon vegetable oil
1 teaspoon cornstarch
1 teaspoon sugar
⅓ cup dry white wine
1 tablespoon lemon juice
2 tablespoons snipped fresh parsley

6 servings

In shallow dish, combine flour, salt and pepper. Dredge veal in flour mixture to coat. Set aside.

In 12-inch nonstick skillet, heat margarine and oil conventionally over medium-high heat. Add veal. Cook 6 to 8 minutes, or until brown on both sides and meat is no longer pink. Place veal on serving platter. Cover to keep warm. Set aside.

In 2-cup measure, combine cornstarch and sugar. Blend in wine and juice. Microwave at High for 2 to 2½ minutes, or until sauce is thickened and translucent, stirring every minute. Stir in parsley. Spoon sauce over veal.

Per Serving: Calories: 187 • Protein: 25 g. • Carbohydrate: 5 g. • Fat: 6 g. • Cholesterol: 88 mg. • Sodium: 147 mg. Exchanges: ¼ starch, 3 lean meat

Squash-stuffed Pork Chops

Sauce:
2 medium tomatoes, peeled, seeded and chopped (2 cups)
½ cup chopped onion
1 clove garlic, minced
1 teaspoon dried oregano leaves
½ teaspoon sugar
¼ teaspoon salt
¼ teaspoon freshly ground pepper

1 medium zucchini squash, sliced (1 cup)
1 medium yellow squash, sliced (1 cup)
1 tablespoon water
6 well-trimmed bone-in pork rib or loin chops (8 oz. each), 1 inch thick
2 teaspoons olive oil
1 teaspoon paprika

6 servings

In 1-quart casserole, combine sauce ingredients. Cover. Microwave at High for 4 to 6 minutes, or until onion is tender-crisp. In food processor or blender, process mixture until smooth. Cover sauce to keep warm. Set aside.

In 1½-quart casserole, combine squashes and water. Cover. Microwave at High for 4 to 6 minutes, or until tender-crisp, stirring once. Drain. Set aside. Cut pocket into one side of each chop. Stuff evenly with squash. Secure with wooden picks. Brush chops evenly with oil. Sprinkle with paprika. Arrange in 10-inch square casserole with thickest portions toward outside. Cover.

Microwave at 70% (Medium High) for 14 to 17 minutes, or until meat is no longer pink, turning chops over and rotating casserole twice. Let stand for 5 minutes before serving. Remove wooden picks. Microwave sauce at High for 1 to 2 minutes, or until hot. Serve with chops. Garnish with snipped fresh parsley, if desired.

Per Serving: Calories: 298 • Protein: 36 g. • Carbohydrate: 7 g. • Fat: 14 g. • Cholesterol: 86 mg. • Sodium: 168 mg.
Exchanges: 4½ lean meat, 1½ vegetable

Apple Chops ▶

1 tablespoon vegetable oil
1 clove garlic, minced
¼ teaspoon seasoned salt
¼ teaspoon freshly ground pepper
4 well-trimmed bone-in pork loin or rib chops (8 oz. each), 1 inch thick
1 medium red cooking apple, cored and sliced
1½ cups pineapple chunks (½-inch chunks)
¾ cup apple cider
1 tablespoon lemon juice
1 tablespoon packed brown sugar
1 tablespoon plus 1 teaspoon cornstarch mixed with 1 tablespoon water

4 servings

In small bowl, combine oil, garlic, salt and pepper. Rub chops evenly with oil mixture. Heat 12-inch nonstick skillet conventionally over medium-high heat. Add chops. Cook for 5 to 6 minutes, or just until meat is browned on both sides. Arrange in 10-inch square casserole with thickest portions toward outside. Spread apple slices and pineapple chunks over chops. In 1-cup measure, combine cider, juice and sugar. Pour over chops. Cover.

Microwave at High for 10 to 12 minutes, or just until meat is no longer pink and apples are tender, rearranging chops once. Using slotted spoon, remove chops and fruit from casserole. Place on serving platter. Cover to keep warm. Set aside.

Pour liquid from casserole into 4-cup measure. Stir in cornstarch mixture. Microwave at High for 1 to 2 minutes, or until sauce is thickened and translucent. Serve with chops.

Per Serving: Calories: 378 • Protein: 35 g. • Carbohydrate: 24 g. • Fat: 16 g. • Cholesterol: 86 mg. • Sodium: 150 mg.
Exchanges: 5 lean meat, 1⅔ fruit

◄ Cashewed Pork Stir-Fry

1 tablespoon plus 1
   teaspoon cornstarch
¼ cup red wine vinegar
2 tablespoons olive oil
2 tablespoons honey
¾ teaspoon ground cumin
¼ teaspoon anise seed
¼ teaspoon crushed red
   pepper flakes
1- lb. well-trimmed pork top
   loin roast, cut into
   2 × ½-inch strips
3 cups snow pea pods
1 cup red pepper chunks
   (1-inch chunks)
1 small onion, cut into thin
   wedges
½ cup whole cashews

4 servings

In 3-quart casserole, combine cornstarch, vinegar, oil, honey, cumin, anise seed and red pepper flakes. Add pork. Toss to coat. Microwave at High for 4 to 6 minutes, or until meat is no longer pink. Stir in pea pods, red pepper and onion. Microwave at High for 6 to 8 minutes, or until onion is tender-crisp, stirring once. Add cashews. Stir to combine. Serve mixture over hot cooked rice, if desired.

Per Serving: Calories: 422 • Protein: 29 g. • Carbohydrate: 24 g. • Fat: 23 g. • Cholesterol: 62 mg. • Sodium: 58 mg. Exchanges: 3¼ medium-fat meat, 2¾ vegetable, ¾ fruit, 1½ fat

Greek Pork Tenderloin

⅓ cup chopped onion
2 teaspoons olive oil
1 clove garlic, minced
½ teaspoon grated lemon peel
4 cups torn spinach leaves
¼ cup crumbled feta cheese
2 teaspoons snipped fresh
   dill weed
1 well-trimmed pork
   tenderloin (approx. 1 lb.)
2 teaspoons lemon juice
¼ teaspoon seasoned salt
¼ teaspoon freshly ground
   pepper

4 servings

In 1½-quart casserole, combine onion, oil, garlic and peel. Microwave at High for 2 to 3 minutes, or until onion is tender-crisp, stirring once. Add spinach. Cover. Microwave at High for 1 to 1½ minutes, or just until spinach is wilted. Add feta and dill weed. Stir to combine. Set aside.

Make horizontal cut through center of tenderloin to within ½ inch of opposite side; do not cut through. Open tenderloin like a book. Spoon and pack spinach mixture down one side of tenderloin. Fold other side over to enclose stuffing. Tie tenderloin at 1½-inch intervals to secure. Brush with juice. Sprinkle evenly with salt and pepper. Place on roasting rack. Cover with wax paper or microwave cooking paper. Microwave at 70% (Medium High) for 8 to 10 minutes, or until meat is no longer pink, rotating rack ¼ turn every 3 minutes. Let stand, covered, for 5 minutes before serving.

Per Serving: Calories: 189 • Protein: 27 g. • Carbohydrate: 4 g. • Fat: 7 g. • Cholesterol: 81 mg. • Sodium: 270 mg. Exchanges: 3¼ lean meat, 1 vegetable

Pork, Pepper ▶
& Cabbage Stir-fry

1 - lb. well-trimmed boneless
    pork top loin roast, cut into
    2 × 1/4-inch strips
3 tablespoons finely chopped
    shallots
1 tablespoon sesame oil
1 teaspoon grated fresh
    gingerroot
3 cups red, yellow and green
    pepper chunks (1-inch
    chunks)
1 medium red onion, thinly
    sliced and separated into
    rings
1 tablespoon rice wine
    vinegar
1 tablespoon soy sauce
1 teaspoon sugar
3 cups coarsely chopped
    white cabbage
1 pkg. (3 oz.) Ramen soup
    mix (discard seasoning
    packet)

4 to 6 servings

In medium mixing bowl, combine
pork, shallots, oil and gingerroot.
Heat 12-inch nonstick skillet
conventionally over medium-
high heat. Add pork mixture to
skillet. Cook for 3 to 4 minutes,
or until meat is no longer pink,
stirring constantly. Remove from
heat. Set aside.

In 3-quart casserole, combine
remaining ingredients, except
cabbage and Ramen noodles.
Cover. Microwave at High for 5
to 7 minutes, or until onion is
tender-crisp, stirring once.

Add cabbage. Toss to combine.
Re-cover. Microwave at High for
2 to 3 minutes, or until hot, stirring once. Using slotted spoon,
add pork and shallots to cabbage
mixture. Toss to combine. Just
before serving, crush noodles
over mixture. Toss to coat.

Per Serving: Calories: 239 • Protein: 19 g.
• Carbohydrate: 16 g. • Fat: 11 g.
• Cholesterol: 42 mg. • Sodium: 303 mg.
Exchanges: 1/2 starch, 2 lean meat,
1 1/2 vegetable, 1 fat

Pork Medallions with Tomatillo Sauce

Tomatillo Sauce (page 81)
1 well-trimmed pork
    tenderloin (approx. 1 lb.),
    cut crosswise into 12 pieces

1/8 teaspoon garlic salt
1/8 teaspoon freshly ground
    pepper
4 Roma tomatoes, sliced

4 servings

Prepare Tomatillo Sauce as directed. Cover to keep warm. Set aside.
Pound pork pieces to 3/4-inch thickness. Sprinkle evenly with salt
and pepper.

Spray 12-inch nonstick skillet with nonstick vegetable cooking spray.
Heat skillet conventionally over medium-high heat. Add pork. Cook
for 4 to 6 minutes, or just until meat is no longer pink, turning over
once. Serve pork with sauce and tomatoes.

Per Serving: Calories: 244 • Protein: 26 g. • Carbohydrate: 11 g. • Fat: 11 g.
• Cholesterol: 74 mg. • Sodium: 123 mg.
Exchanges: 3 lean meat, 2 vegetable, 1/4 fat

Asparagus Rissoto

1	cup uncooked arborio rice
¾	cup chopped yellow pepper
¼	cup margarine or butter
12	oz. asparagus spears, cut into 1-inch lengths (1½ cups)
2¼	cups hot water
½	cup dry sherry
¼	cup snipped sorrel leaves
¼	teaspoon garlic powder
¼	teaspoon salt
¼	teaspoon freshly ground pepper
2	cups cubed fully cooked lean ham (½-inch cubes)
¼	cup shredded fresh Parmesan cheese

4 servings

In 3-quart casserole, combine rice, yellow pepper and margarine. Microwave at High for 5 to 7 minutes, or until pepper is tender, stirring in asparagus after 3 minutes.

Add water, sherry, sorrel, garlic powder, salt and pepper. Microwave at High for 15 to 19 minutes, or until rice is tender and most of liquid is absorbed, stirring twice.

Add ham and Parmesan cheese. Stir to combine. Cover. Let stand for 5 minutes before serving.

Per Serving: Calories: 469 • Protein: 24 g. • Carbohydrate: 47 g. • Fat: 20 g.
• Cholesterol: 47 mg. • Sodium: 1467 mg.
Exchanges: 2¼ starch, 2 medium-fat meat, 2 vegetable, 2 fat

Cherried Ham Steak ▲

1½-	lb. well-trimmed fully cooked bone-in lean ham steak, ¾ inch thick
2	cups fresh whole bing, Lambert or Rainier cherries, pitted
⅓	cup sugar
¼	cup orange juice
1	teaspoon grated lime peel
¼	cup lime juice
1	tablespoon plus 1 teaspoon cornstarch

4 servings

Place ham steak in 10-inch square casserole. Set aside. In medium mixing bowl, combine remaining ingredients. Pour mixture over ham steak. Cover. Microwave at High for 10 to 15 minutes, or until sauce is thickened and translucent, stirring sauce and rotating dish twice. Garnish with additional grated lime peel, if desired.

Per Serving: Calories: 340 • Protein: 31 g.
• Carbohydrate: 35 g. • Fat: 8 g.
• Cholesterol: 73 mg. • Sodium: 2225 mg.
Exchanges: 4½ lean meat, 2⅓ fruit

Ham & Pineapple Pie

  1 tablespoon yellow cornmeal
  1 cup all-purpose flour
  1 tablespoon poppy seed
1½ teaspoons baking powder
  1 teaspoon fennel seed
  ½ teaspoon salt
  1 tablespoon margarine or butter
  ¼ to ⅓ cup milk
  1 cup shredded mozzarella cheese
  1 cup finely chopped fully cooked lean ham
  1 cup pineapple chunks (¾-inch chunks)
  ¼ cup diagonally sliced green onions
  2 tablespoons finely chopped red pepper
    (optional)
  2 tablespoons shredded fresh Parmesan
    cheese
  1 tablespoon snipped fresh parsley

4 to 6 servings

Per Serving: Calories: 235 • Protein: 13 g. • Carbohydrate: 22 g.
• Fat: 10 g. • Cholesterol: 32 mg. • Sodium: 787 mg.
Exchanges: 1¼ starch, 1¼ medium-fat meat, ¼ fruit, ¾ fat

Spray 9-inch pie plate with nonstick vegetable cooking spray. Sprinkle evenly with cornmeal. Set aside.

In medium mixing bowl, combine flour, poppy seed, baking powder, fennel seed and salt. Add margarine. At low speed of electric mixer, blend until mixture resembles coarse crumbs. Gradually stir in enough milk to make stiff dough.

Turn dough out onto lightly floured surface. Knead for 1 to 2 minutes, or until smooth. Roll dough into 9-inch circle. Ease into prepared pie plate, pressing up side as necessary; do not cover rim. Sprinkle mozzarella cheese evenly over bottom of crust. Top evenly with remaining ingredients.

Microwave at High for 6 to 8 minutes, or until center is hot, crust feels light and springy to the touch, and no unbaked dough is visible through bottom of pie plate, rotating ¼ turn every 2 minutes. Let stand directly on counter for 5 to 10 minutes before serving.

Beet Pasta

2 medium beets, unpeeled, stems removed
1/2 cup hot water
1/2 teaspoon salt
   Basic Fresh Pasta (below)

4 servings

Place beets in 1 1/2-quart casserole. In 1-cup measure, combine water and salt. Stir until salt is dissolved. Add to beets. Cover. Microwave at High for 13 to 15 minutes, or until beets are tender, turning beets over and rotating dish every 5 minutes. Let stand, covered, for 3 to 5 minutes, or until beets are cool enough to handle.

Peel, trim and cut up beets. In food processor or blender, process beets until finely chopped. Set aside. Prepare pasta as directed, except stir in beets with eggs.

NOTE: Beet pasta loses some color when cooked. For less color loss, allow pasta to dry for at least 2 hours. The drier the pasta, the less color loss.

Per Serving: Calories: 251 • Protein: 9 g. • Carbohydrate: 45 g.
• Fat: 3 g. • Cholesterol: 106 mg. • Sodium: 330 mg.
Exchanges: 2 1/2 starch, 1/2 medium-fat meat, 1/2 vegetable

Tomato Pasta

2 medium tomatoes, peeled, seeded and
   coarsely chopped (2 cups)
   Basic Fresh Pasta (below)

4 servings

Place tomatoes in 1-quart casserole. Cover. Microwave at High for 3 to 4 minutes, or until hot. Strain juice through cheesecloth. Discard juice. Prepare pasta as directed, except stir in tomato pulp with eggs.

Per Serving: Calories: 255 • Protein: 10 g. • Carbohydrate: 46 g.
• Fat: 3 g. • Cholesterol: 106 mg. • Sodium: 41 mg.
Exchanges: 2 1/2 starch, 1/2 medium-fat meat, 3/4 vegetable

Spinach Pasta ▶

8 cups torn spinach leaves
   Basic Fresh Pasta (below)

4 servings

Place spinach in 3-quart casserole. Cover. Microwave at High for 2 to 3 minutes, or just until wilted, stirring once. Drain, pressing with back of spoon to remove excess moisture. Chop fine. Prepare pasta as directed, except stir in spinach with eggs.

Per Serving: Calories: 261 • Protein: 12 g. • Carbohydrate: 46 g.
• Fat: 3 g. • Cholesterol: 106 mg. • Sodium: 121 mg.
Exchanges: 2 1/2 starch, 1/2 medium-fat meat, 1 1/4 vegetable

Basic Fresh Pasta

1 1/2 to 2 cups all-purpose flour,
   divided
2 eggs
1/4 teaspoon garlic powder
   (optional)

4 servings

Per Serving: Calories: 236 • Protein: 9 g.
• Carbohydrate: 42 g. • Fat: 3 g.
• Cholesterol: 106 mg. • Sodium: 33 mg.
Exchanges: 2 1/2 starch, 1/2 medium-fat meat

How to Make Basic Fresh Pasta

Combine 1 cup flour, the eggs and garlic powder in medium mixing bowl. Mix well with fork. Stir in enough additional flour to make soft dough. Form dough into ball.

Place dough on lightly floured surface. Knead for 5 to 10 minutes, or until smooth and elastic, adding flour as necessary to reduce stickiness. Cover with light cloth. Let stand for 30 minutes.

Divide dough into thirds. On lightly floured surface, roll one third into 16 x 10-inch rectangle. Sprinkle lightly with flour to prevent sticking. Fold dough loosely from two opposite sides, working to center.

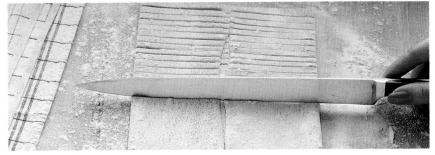

Slice crosswise with sharp knife at ¼-inch intervals. Slide blade of knife lengthwise under dough and lift to unfold. Spread pasta strips in single layer on clean cloth. Repeat with remaining dough. Let dry, uncovered, for 1 to 2 hours. Heat 3 quarts water conventionally over high heat until boiling. Add pasta and stir. Cook for 4 to 5 minutes, or until pasta is tender. Drain. Serve with pasta toppings on pages 116 to 119.

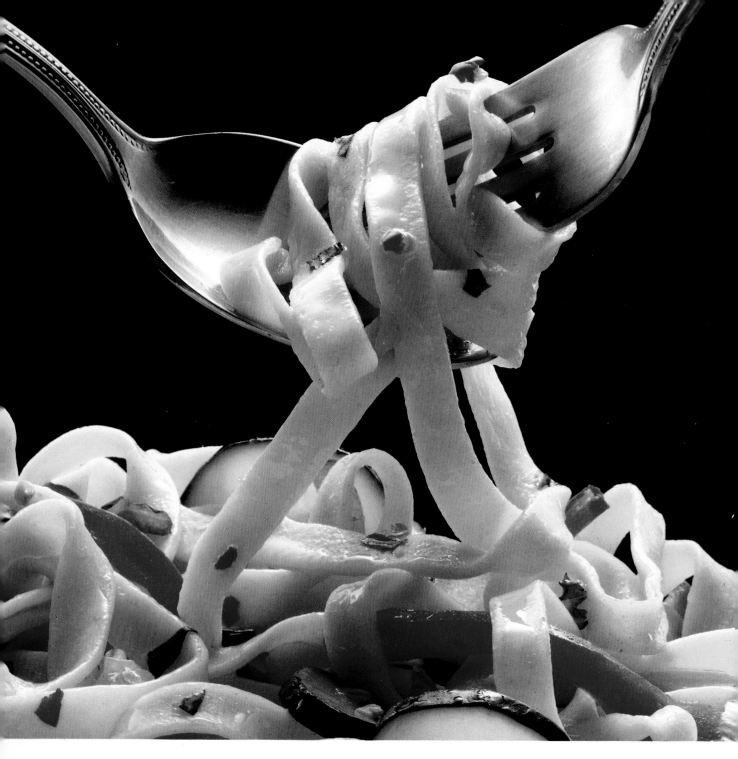

Zucchini Pepper Pasta

¼ cup chopped shallots
3 tablespoons olive oil
1 clove garlic, minced
¼ teaspoon salt
⅛ to ¼ teaspoon crushed red pepper flakes
3 medium zucchini, sliced (3 cups)
1 medium red pepper, cut into thin strips
¼ cup dry white wine
¼ cup snipped fresh basil leaves
   Cooked fresh pasta (pages 114 to 115)

In 2-quart casserole, combine shallots, oil, garlic, salt and red pepper flakes. Microwave at High for 2 to 3 minutes, or until shallots are tender, stirring once. Add zucchini, red pepper and wine. Mix well. Cover. Microwave at High for 7 to 9 minutes, or until zucchini is tender. Stir in basil. Add to hot pasta. Toss to combine.

Per Serving: Calories: 130 • Protein: 2 g. • Carbohydrate: 7 g.
• Fat: 10 g. • Cholesterol: 0 • Sodium: 141 mg.
Exchanges: 1¼ vegetable, 2 fat

4 servings

Arugula & Olive Toss

    1 wheel (4½ oz.) Camembert or Brie cheese,
       3 x 1 inches
    2 medium tomatoes, seeded and coarsely
       chopped (2 cups)
    1 cup whole Kalamata (Greek) olives, pitted,
       cut into quarters, rinsed and drained
    ¼ cup olive oil
    1 tablespoon grated lemon peel
    1 clove garlic, minced
    ½ teaspoon sugar
    ½ teaspoon coarsely ground pepper
    2 cups torn arugula leaves, stems removed
       Cooked fresh pasta (pages 114 to 115)

4 servings

Freeze Camembert 1 hour. Cut off and discard rind. Thinly slice cheese. Set aside.

In 2-quart casserole, combine remaining ingredients, except cheese, arugula and pasta. Microwave at High for 4 to 5 minutes, or until hot, stirring once. Stir in cheese and arugula. Add to hot pasta. Toss to combine.

Per Serving: Calories: 362 • Protein: 8 g. • Carbohydrate: 9 g. • Fat: 34 g. • Cholesterol: 23 mg. • Sodium: 1468 mg.
Exchanges: 1 high-fat meat, 1¾ vegetable, 5 fat

Fresh Herb Pesto

    1 cup watercress leaves
    ¼ cup pine nuts
    ¼ cup shredded fresh Parmesan cheese
    1 clove garlic, minced
    1 teaspoon grated lemon peel
    ¼ cup olive oil
       Cooked fresh pasta (pages 114 to 115)

4 servings

In food processor or blender, combine all ingredients, except pasta. Process until smooth. Add pesto to hot pasta. Toss to coat. If desired, add halved cherry tomatoes to pasta.

Variation 1: Prepare as directed, except substitute finely torn spinach leaves, slivered almonds and crumbled feta cheese for watercress, pine nuts and Parmesan cheese.

Variation 2: Prepare as directed, except substitute fresh cilantro leaves and shredded Monterey Jack cheese for watercress and Parmesan cheese. Omit garlic and lemon peel. Add 2 to 3 teaspoons finely chopped seeded jalapeño pepper.

Per Serving: Calories: 196 • Protein: 5 g. • Carbohydrate: 2 g. • Fat: 20 g. • Cholesterol: 5 mg. • Sodium: 118 mg.
Exchanges: ½ high-fat meat, ¼ vegetable, 3 fat

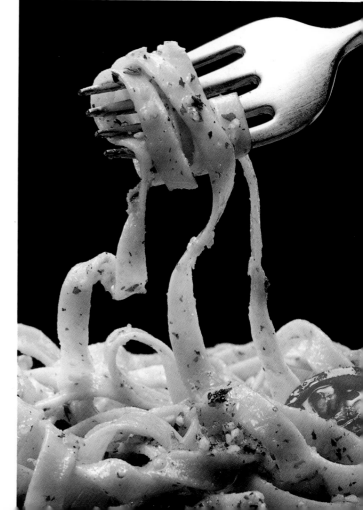

Asparagus-Tomato Toss

- 1 lb. asparagus spears, cut into 1-inch lengths (2 cups)
- 2 tablespoons plus 1 teaspoon olive oil, divided
- 1/2 teaspoon fennel seed
- 1 medium tomato, seeded and chopped (1 cup)
- 2 teaspoons lemon juice
  Cooked fresh pasta (pages 114 to 115)

4 servings

In 2-quart casserole, combine asparagus, 1 teaspoon oil and the fennel seed. Cover. Microwave at High for 6 to 8 minutes, or until asparagus is tender, stirring once. Drain. Add remaining 2 tablespoons oil, the tomato and juice to casserole. Mix well. Add asparagus mixture to hot pasta. Toss to combine.

Per Serving: Calories: 105 • Protein: 4 g. • Carbohydrate: 7 g.
• Fat: 8 g. • Cholesterol: 0 • Sodium: 7 mg.
Exchanges: 1 1/4 vegetable, 1 3/4 fat

Chervil Alfredo Sauce

- 2 tablespoons all-purpose flour
- 1 clove garlic, minced
- 1/4 teaspoon salt
- 1/4 teaspoon freshly ground pepper
- 1 cup milk
- 3 oz. chèvre cheese (goat cheese), crumbled (1/2 cup)
- 1/4 cup snipped fresh chervil leaves
  Cooked fresh pasta (pages 114 to 115)

4 servings

In 4-cup measure, combine flour, garlic, salt and pepper. Blend in milk. Microwave at High for 4 to 5 minutes, or until sauce thickens and bubbles, stirring every minute. Add chèvre. Stir until cheese is melted. Stir in chervil. Serve over hot pasta.

Per Serving: Calories: 129 • Protein: 7 g. • Carbohydrate: 7 g.
• Fat: 8 g. • Cholesterol: 25 mg. • Sodium: 275 mg.
Exchanges: 1/4 starch, 3/4 high-fat meat, 1/4 low-fat milk, 1/2 fat

Mushroom-Olive Sauce

    8 oz. mushrooms, cut into quarters (3 cups)
   ½ cup halved stuffed green olives, rinsed and
       drained
   ⅓ cup roasted red peppers, drained, cut into
       thin strips
   ¼ cup snipped fresh parsley
    3 tablespoons olive oil
       Cooked fresh pasta (pages 114 to 115)

4 servings

Place mushrooms in 2-quart casserole. Cover.
Microwave at High for 5 to 6 minutes, or just until
tender, stirring once. Drain.

Stir in olives, red peppers, parsley and oil.
Re-cover. Let stand for 5 minutes. Serve over
hot pasta.

Per Serving: Calories: 128 • Protein: 2 g. • Carbohydrate: 4 g.
• Fat: 13 g. • Cholesterol: 0 • Sodium: 412 mg.
Exchanges: ¾ vegetable, 2½ fat

Fresh Tomato Sauce

    3 medium tomatoes, cut into 1-inch cubes
       (3½ cups)
    1 small onion, chopped (1 cup)
    1 can (6 oz.) tomato paste
   ½ cup dry red wine
   ¼ cup chopped fresh Italian parsley leaves
    3 anchovy fillets, finely chopped
    1 clove garlic, minced
    1 teaspoon instant beef bouillon granules
   ½ teaspoon sugar
       Cooked fresh pasta (pages 114 to 115)

4 servings

In 3-quart casserole, combine all ingredients,
except pasta. Cover. Microwave at High for 5 minutes. Stir. Reduce power to 50% (Medium). Microwave, uncovered, for 24 to 30 minutes longer, or
until sauce is slightly thickened, stirring 2 or 3 times.
Serve over hot pasta.

Per Serving: Calories: 116 • Protein: 5 g. • Carbohydrate: 20 g.
• Fat: 1 g. • Cholesterol: 2 mg. • Sodium: 674 mg.
Exchanges: 4 vegetable, ¼ fat

Fresh Desserts & Breads

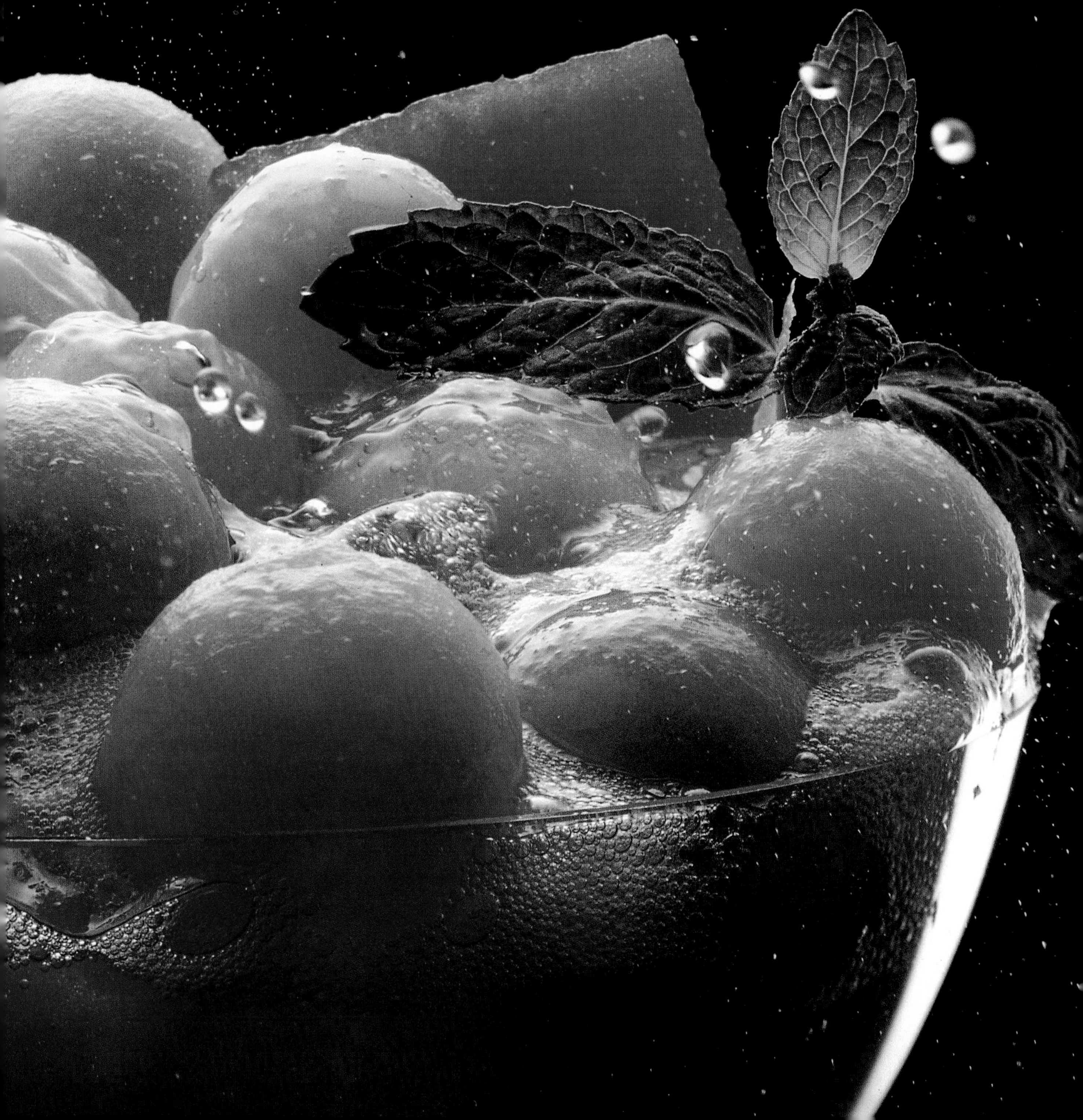

Old-fashioned Plum Cobbler ▼

- 8 to 10 plums, peeled, pitted and sliced (3 cups)
- 2/3 cup plus 1 tablespoon sugar, divided
- 1¾ cups plus 1 tablespoon all-purpose flour, divided
- ½ teaspoon salt
- 3 teaspoons baking powder
- ½ cup margarine or butter, cut into small pieces, divided
- 1 cup milk
- ¾ teaspoon ground cinnamon
- ⅛ teaspoon ground nutmeg

6 to 8 servings

In 2-quart casserole, combine plums, 2/3 cup sugar and 1 tablespoon flour. Toss to coat. Microwave at High for 8 to 10 minutes, or until mixture comes to a boil, stirring twice. Set aside, covered, to keep warm.

Heat conventional oven to 425°F. In large mixing bowl, combine remaining 1 tablespoon sugar and 1¾ cups flour, the salt and baking powder. Add ¼ cup plus 2 tablespoons margarine to mixture. Beat at low speed of electric mixer until particles resemble coarse crumbs. Add milk. Stir just until moistened.

Drop dough by heaping tablespoons over hot fruit mixture. Sprinkle evenly with cinnamon and nutmeg. Dot with remaining 2 tablespoons margarine. Bake for 20 to 25 minutes, or until topping is light golden brown. Serve warm with whipped cream or ice cream, if desired.

Per Serving: Calories: 330 • Protein: 5 g. • Carbohydrate: 50 g. • Fat: 13 g. • Cholesterol: 4 mg. • Sodium: 446 mg.
Exchanges: 1½ starch, 1⅔ fruit, 2½ fat

Cherry Clafoutis

- 1 lb. bing cherries, stems removed*
- 1½ teaspoons grated orange peel, divided
- 1 cup sugar
- ¼ cup margarine or butter, softened
- ¼ cup sour cream
- 2 eggs, beaten
- 2 tablespoons kirsch (cherry-flavored liqueur)
- 1 cup all-purpose flour
- 1 teaspoon baking powder
- ⅛ teaspoon salt

6 servings

Spray 10-inch deep-dish pie plate with nonstick vegetable cooking spray. Arrange cherries in single layer in bottom of plate. Sprinkle evenly with 1 teaspoon peel. Set aside.

In medium mixing bowl, combine sugar, margarine and sour cream. Beat at high speed of electric mixer until fluffy. Blend in eggs and kirsch. Add remaining ingredients, except remaining peel. Beat at low speed of electric mixer until smooth. Pour mixture over cherries. Sprinkle top evenly with remaining ½ teaspoon peel.

Microwave at 70% (Medium High) for 21 to 30 minutes, or until wooden pick inserted in center comes out clean, rotating every 7 minutes. Sprinkle with sifted powdered sugar, if desired.

*In a traditional clafoutis, cherries are not pitted.

Per Serving: Calories: 375 • Protein: 5 g. • Carbohydrate: 63 g. • Fat: 12 g. • Cholesterol: 75 mg. • Sodium: 233 mg.
Exchanges: 1 starch, ⅓ medium-fat meat, 3¼ fruit, 2 fat

Grape-Raspberry Tart

Crust:

- 1 cup all-purpose flour
- 3 tablespoons packed brown sugar
- 1/4 teaspoon salt
- 1/4 cup plus 2 tablespoons margarine or butter, softened
- 1 egg yolk
- 2 teaspoons grated orange peel
- 1 tablespoon orange juice
- 1/2 teaspoon vanilla

- 1 pkg. (8 oz.) cream cheese, softened
- 1/4 cup granulated sugar
- 1 tablespoon milk
- 1 1/2 cups seedless green grapes
- 1 cup red raspberries

6 servings

In medium mixing bowl, combine flour, brown sugar and salt. Add margarine. Beat at low speed of electric mixer until particles resemble coarse crumbs. Add remaining crust ingredients, mixing with fork until particles are moistened and cling together. Form dough into ball. Wrap in plastic wrap. Chill at least 30 minutes.

Place dough on lightly floured surface. Roll into 12-inch circle. Fit circle into 9-inch pie plate. Flute edges. Prick bottom of crust with fork at 1/2-inch intervals. Microwave at High for 5 to 7 minutes, or until crust is dry and opaque, rotating 2 or 3 times. Cool completely.

In medium mixing bowl, combine cream cheese, granulated sugar and milk. Beat at medium speed of electric mixer until fluffy. Spread mixture in bottom of crust. Arrange grapes and raspberries in single layer on cream cheese. Chill at least 2 hours before serving.

Variation: Substitute other fruit, such as blueberries, cherries, plum halves, apricot halves, sliced kiwifruit or sliced bananas, for grapes and raspberries.

Per Serving: Calories: 420 • Protein: 6 g. • Carbohydrate: 42 g. • Fat: 26 g.
• Cholesterol: 77 mg. • Sodium: 341 mg.
Exchanges: 1 starch, 1/2 medium-fat meat, 1 3/4 fruit, 4 3/4 fat

Apple Dumplings with Cran-Apple Glaze

Pastry:
- 2 cups all-purpose flour
- 1 teaspoon salt
- ³/₄ cup shortening
- 3 to 4 tablespoons water

- ³/₄ cup coarsely chopped cranberries
- ¹/₃ cup chopped walnuts
- 2 tablespoons granulated sugar

- ³/₄ teaspoon ground cinnamon
- ¹/₄ teaspoon ground cloves
- 6 medium cooking apples, peeled and cored
- ¹/₂ cup packed brown sugar
- 1 tablespoon plus 1 teaspoon cornstarch
- ³/₄ cup cranberry-apple juice

6 servings

Heat conventional oven to 425°F. In large mixing bowl, combine flour and salt. Add shortening. Beat at low speed of electric mixer until particles resemble coarse crumbs. Sprinkle with water, 1 tablespoon at a time, mixing with fork until particles are moistened and cling together. Form dough into ball. Place on lightly floured surface. Roll out two-thirds of dough into 14-inch square. Cut into four 7-inch squares. Roll remaining dough into 14 × 7-inch rectangle. Cut into two 7-inch squares. Set aside.

In medium mixing bowl, combine cranberries, walnuts, granulated sugar, cinnamon and cloves. Stuff apples evenly with cranberry mixture. Place 1 apple in center of each pastry square. Bring corners of each square up over apples, pinching sides together to seal. Turn corners of dough down, leaving centers of apples exposed.

Spray 10-inch square casserole with nonstick vegetable cooking spray. Place apples in prepared casserole. Bake for 45 to 50 minutes, or until pastry is golden brown and apples are tender. In 4-cup measure, combine brown sugar and cornstarch. Blend in juice. Microwave at High for 3¹/₂ to 5 minutes, or until mixture is thickened and translucent, stirring after 2 minutes and then every minute. Just before serving, spoon glaze evenly over dumplings.

Per Serving: Calories: 635 • Protein: 6 g. • Carbohydrate: 88 g. • Fat: 31 g.
• Cholesterol: 0 • Sodium: 376 mg.
Exchanges: 2 starch, 3³/₄ fruit, 6 fat

◀ Bluebarb Pie

- 1¹/₂ cups all-purpose flour
- ¹/₂ teaspoon salt
- ¹/₂ cup shortening
- 2 to 3 tablespoons water

Filling:
- 2 cups sliced rhubarb (³/₄-inch lengths)
- 2 cups blueberries
- 1¹/₃ cups granulated sugar
- ¹/₃ cup all-purpose flour
- 2 teaspoons grated fresh gingerroot

- 2 tablespoons packed brown sugar

6 servings

Heat conventional oven to 425°F. In medium mixing bowl, combine flour and salt. Add shortening. Beat at low speed of electric mixer until particles resemble coarse crumbs. Reserve ³/₄ cup crumbs. Set aside.

Sprinkle water, 1 tablespoon at a time, over remaining flour mixture, mixing with fork until particles are moistened and cling together. Form dough into ball. Place on lightly floured surface. Roll dough into 12-inch circle. Fit circle into 9-inch pie plate. Flute edges. Set aside.

In large mixing bowl, combine filling ingredients. Spoon into crust. Microwave at High for 8 to 10 minutes, or until fruit is tender-crisp and hot, rotating once. In small bowl, combine reserved crumbs and brown sugar. Sprinkle mixture evenly over top of pie. Bake conventionally for 20 to 25 minutes, or until crust is golden brown.

Per Serving: Calories: 514 • Protein: 5 g.
• Carbohydrate: 86 g. • Fat: 18 g.
• Cholesterol: 0 • Sodium: 189 mg.
Exchanges: 2 starch, 3³/₄ fruit, 3¹/₄ fat

Apple Pizza

Sauce:

- 3 medium apricots, pitted and quartered
- 1/2 teaspoon grated lemon peel
- 1 tablespoon lemon juice
- 1/3 cup sugar
- 1 1/2 teaspoons cornstarch mixed with 1 tablespoon water

Crust:

- 2 cups all-purpose flour
- 1/4 teaspoon salt
- 1/2 cup margarine or butter, cut into small pieces
- 1/4 cup sugar
- 2 eggs, beaten
- 1 teaspoon vanilla

- 3 cups water
- 2 tablespoons lemon juice
- 2 medium cooking apples, cored and thinly sliced
- 2 tablespoons margarine or butter, melted
- 1 tablespoon sugar
- 1/4 teaspoon ground cinnamon
- 1/4 cup sliced almonds

8 servings

In 1-quart casserole, combine apricots, peel and juice. Cover. Microwave at High for 3 to 5 minutes, or until apricots are tender, stirring once. In food processor or blender, process mixture until smooth. Return to casserole. Stir in 1/3 cup sugar. Microwave at 50% (Medium) for 45 seconds to 1 minute, or until very hot. Stir in cornstarch mixture. Microwave at High for 1 to 1 1/2 minutes, or until sauce is thickened and translucent, stirring every 30 seconds. Chill.

In medium mixing bowl, combine flour and salt. Add cut-up margarine. Beat at low speed of electric mixer until particles resemble coarse crumbs. Stir in remaining crust ingredients. Form dough into ball. Wrap in plastic wrap. Chill 1 hour.

Heat conventional oven to 400°F. In medium mixing bowl, combine water and juice. Immerse apple slices in water mixture to prevent discoloring. Set aside. Place dough on lightly floured surface. Roll into 12-inch circle. Place circle on 12-inch nonstick pizza pan. Press dough into pan. Spread sauce on crust to within 1/2 inch of edge.

Drain apples. Arrange over sauce. Brush apples with melted margarine. Sprinkle evenly with remaining ingredients. Bake for 20 to 25 minutes, or until crust is golden brown. Serve in wedges.

Per Serving: Calories: 370 • Protein: 6 g. • Carbohydrate: 48 g. • Fat: 18 g. • Cholesterol: 53 mg. • Sodium: 252 mg.
Exchanges: 1 3/4 starch, 1 1/2 fruit, 3 1/2 fat

Lemon Soufflé Cake with Strawberries

3 tablespoons all-purpose flour

⅓ cup granulated sugar

¼ cup milk

4 eggs, separated

1 tablespoon grated lemon peel

2 teaspoons vanilla

¼ teaspoon cream of tartar

2 teaspoons Grand Marnier or other orange-flavored liqueur

⅓ cup crème fraîche*

2 teaspoons packed brown sugar or granulated brown sugar

2 cups sliced strawberries

6 servings

*To make crème fraîche, combine ¼ cup whipping cream and ¼ cup sour cream in small bowl. Refrigerate overnight, or until thick, stirring occasionally.

Lightly butter 10-inch square casserole. Line with 16 × 10-inch sheet of lightly buttered wax paper, with long ends hanging over edges. Set aside. In 2-cup measure, combine flour and sugar. Blend in milk. Microwave at High for 1½ to 2 minutes, or until mixture thickens, stirring every 30 seconds. Spoon mixture into medium mixing bowl. Add egg yolks, peel and vanilla. Whisk until smooth. Set aside.

In second medium mixing bowl, combine egg whites and cream of tartar. Beat at high speed of electric mixer until stiff but not dry. Fold whites into yolk mixture. Spread mixture in prepared casserole. Microwave at 30% (Medium Low) for 19 to 26 minutes, or until wooden pick inserted in center comes out clean. Invert casserole over serving platter. Let stand for 5 minutes. Pull wax paper to loosen soufflé. Remove casserole. Chill soufflé at least 15 minutes.

Trim edges of soufflé. Sprinkle soufflé with Grand Marnier. Spread crème fraîche evenly over soufflé. Sprinkle evenly with brown sugar. Top with strawberries, arranged in single layer. Sprinkle with sifted powdered sugar, if desired.

Per Serving: Calories: 197 • Protein: 6 g. • Carbohydrate: 21 g. • Fat: 10 g. • Cholesterol: 160 mg. • Sodium: 63 mg.
Exchanges: ½ medium-fat meat, 1½ fruit, 1½ fat

Lemon Pudding Cake

  2 eggs, separated
½ cup milk
  1 teaspoon grated lemon peel
⅓ cup lemon juice
½ cup sugar
¼ cup all-purpose flour
⅛ teaspoon salt
¼ teaspoon poppy seed

4 servings

Spray 1-quart casserole with nonstick vegetable cooking spray. Set aside. In small mixing bowl, beat egg yolks at low speed of electric mixer. At low speed, blend in milk, peel and juice, then beat in sugar, flour and salt. Set aside.

In second small mixing bowl, beat egg whites at high speed of electric mixer until stiff but not dry. Fold whites into yolk mixture. Pour mixture into prepared casserole. With rubber spatula, smooth surface. If desired, make peaks in surface for decoration. Sprinkle poppy seed evenly over top.

Microwave at 50% (Medium) for 15 to 18 minutes, or until surface is dry and pudding is set, rotating dish ¼ turn every 3 minutes.

Let stand for 10 minutes. Serve warm. Garnish with additional grated peel or sliced almonds, if desired.

Per Serving: Calories: 188 • Protein: 5 g.
• Carbohydrate: 34 g. • Fat: 4 g.
• Cholesterol: 111 mg. • Sodium: 120 mg.
Exchanges: ¼ starch, ½ medium-fat meat, 2 fruit, ⅓ fat

Pineapple Pudding Cake ▲

  2 eggs, separated
½ cup milk
½ cup sugar
¼ cup all-purpose flour
⅛ teaspoon salt
¾ cup finely chopped pineapple
¼ cup toasted fresh coconut curls*

4 to 5 servings

Spray 1½-quart casserole with nonstick vegetable cooking spray. Set aside. In small mixing bowl, beat egg yolks at low speed of electric mixer. At low speed, blend in milk, then beat in sugar, flour and salt. Stir in pineapple. Set aside.

In second small mixing bowl, beat egg whites at high speed of electric mixer until stiff but not dry. Fold whites into pineapple mixture. Pour mixture into prepared casserole. With rubber spatula, smooth surface. Microwave at 50% (Medium) for 18 to 21 minutes, or until surface is dry and pudding is set, rotating dish ¼ turn every 3 minutes. Let stand for 10 minutes. Serve warm. Sprinkle coconut curls evenly over top.

*To make toasted fresh coconut curls, heat conventional oven to 375°F. Pierce the three shiny black "eyes" at top of coconut with ice pick or screwdriver; drain and discard liquid. Split coconut open by hitting it several times with a hammer. Pull husk away from meat. Using vegetable peeler, remove thin strips of coconut meat. Spread strips evenly on large baking sheet. Bake for 5 to 7 minutes, or until light golden brown, stirring once or twice.

Per Serving: Calories: 171 • Protein: 4 g. • Carbohydrate: 30 g. • Fat: 5 g.
• Cholesterol: 88 mg. • Sodium: 94 mg.
Exchanges: ⅓ starch, ½ medium-fat meat, 1½ fruit, ½ fat

Pear Bread Pudding with Brandied Praline Sauce

Pear Mixture:

- ⅓ cup granulated sugar
- ⅓ cup dry red wine
- ¼ cup water
- 2 teaspoons lemon juice
- 2 lemon slices
- ⅛ teaspoon ground cinnamon
- ⅛ teaspoon ground nutmeg
- 3 medium red pears, cored and sliced

Pudding Mixture:

- 2½ cups milk
- 4 eggs, beaten
- 4 cups dry French bread cubes (1-inch cubes)
- ⅓ cup granulated sugar
- 2 tablespoons cornstarch
- 1 teaspoon vanilla
- ½ teaspoon ground cinnamon
- ⅛ teaspoon ground nutmeg
- ⅛ teaspoon salt

Sauce:

- ½ cup packed brown sugar
- ½ cup margarine or butter
- ¼ cup brandy

6 to 8 servings

In 3-quart casserole, combine all pear mixture ingredients, except pears. Cover. Microwave at High for 3½ to 5 minutes, or until mixture comes to a boil. Add pears. Mix well. Re-cover. Microwave at High for 6 to 8 minutes, or until pears are tender, stirring twice. Set aside.

In 4-cup measure, microwave milk at High for 4 to 6 minutes, or until hot but not boiling. Beat eggs into hot milk. Drain and discard poaching liquid from pears. Remove and discard lemon slices. Add remaining pudding mixture ingredients to pears. Gradually stir in hot milk mixture.

Microwave at 50% (Medium) for 10 to 15 minutes, or until almost set in center, gently pushing outer edges toward center every 3 minutes. Do not overcook. Let stand on countertop for at least 30 minutes before serving.

In 4-cup measure, combine sauce ingredients. Microwave at High for 1 to 2 minutes, or until margarine is almost melted. Stir with whisk until smooth. Microwave at High for 2½ to 3 minutes, or until mixture comes to a boil. Let boil for 1 minute. Stir again with whisk. Spoon pudding into individual serving dishes. Drizzle sauce evenly over each serving. Garnish with chopped walnuts, if desired.

NOTE: Pudding may be served warm or cold.

Per Serving: Calories: 402 • Protein: 8 g. • Carbohydrate: 51 g. • Fat: 17 g. • Cholesterol: 117 mg. • Sodium: 344 mg.
Exchanges: ¾ starch, ½ medium-fat meat, 2⅓ fruit, ⅓ low-fat milk, 3 fat

Grand Marnier Dessert

¼ cup sugar
1 tablespoon cornstarch
2 teaspoons grated orange peel
1 cup orange juice
¼ cup Grand Marnier or other orange-flavored liqueur
4 to 5 medium seedless oranges

¼ cup golden raisins

Topping:
3 oz. white baking chocolate, grated
1 tablespoon half-and-half
1 tablespoon margarine or butter

6 servings

In 4-cup measure, combine sugar, cornstarch and peel. Blend in juice and Grand Marnier. Microwave at High for 4 to 6 minutes, or until sauce is thickened and translucent, stirring after 2 minutes and then every minute. Cool slightly.

Peel and section oranges as directed at right. Pour sauce over oranges. Toss to coat. Cover. Chill 45 minutes. Spoon oranges into individual serving dishes. Sprinkle raisins evenly in center of each dish. Set aside.

In 2-cup measure, combine topping ingredients. Microwave at 50% (Medium) for 1 to 1½ minutes, or until chocolate is melted and mixture can be stirred smooth, stirring once. Drizzle about 1 tablespoon topping over each dessert. Serve immediately.

Per Serving: Calories: 252 • Protein: 2 g. • Carbohydrate: 44 g. • Fat: 7 g.
• Cholesterol: 3 mg. • Sodium: 36 mg.
Exchanges: 1 starch, 2 fruit, 1⅓ fat

How to Peel & Section Oranges

Remove peel and white membrane from oranges with sharp knife. Hold fruit over medium mixing bowl to catch juice.

Cut to center between fruit segments and divide membranes, releasing fruit into bowl.

129

Broiled Exotic Fruit with White Chocolate Sauce

½ cup sugar
2 tablespoons all-purpose flour
⅛ teaspoon salt
⅓ cup half-and-half
1 tablespoon margarine or butter, melted
1 tablespoon light corn syrup
3 oz. white baking chocolate, grated
1 teaspoon vanilla
1 medium Asian pear, cored and sliced
1 mango, peeled and sliced
1 medium carambola (star fruit), sliced
3 Black Mission figs, sliced

4 to 6 servings

In 4-cup measure, combine sugar, flour and salt. Blend in half-and-half, margarine and corn syrup. Microwave at High for 2 to 3 minutes, or until mixture comes to a boil, stirring twice. Stir in chocolate and vanilla. Microwave at High for 30 seconds to 1 minute, or until chocolate is melted and sauce can be stirred smooth, stirring once. Pour into serving bowl. Cover to keep warm. Set aside.

Line conventional broiler pan with foil. Arrange fruits in single layer on prepared pan. Place under conventional broiler, with surface of fruits 4 to 6 inches from heat. Broil for 5 to 7 minutes per side, or until fruits are very hot and lightly browned.

Arrange on serving platter. Serve sauce as dip for fruits or spoon over fruits.

Per Serving: Calories: 270 • Protein: 2 g.
• Carbohydrate: 49 g. • Fat: 8 g.
• Cholesterol: 7 mg. • Sodium: 92 mg.
Exchanges: 1 starch, 2 fruit, 1⅔ fat

Poached Peaches with Caramel Sauce ▲

1 can (5½ oz.) apricot nectar (⅔ cup)
⅓ cup granulated sugar
¼ cup apricot-flavored brandy
¼ cup water
½ teaspoon ground cinnamon
¼ teaspoon ground ginger
4 medium peaches, peeled*, pitted and sliced
¼ cup packed brown sugar
2 tablespoons all-purpose flour
½ cup whipping cream
1 tablespoon dark corn syrup
2 tablespoons margarine or butter
1 teaspoon vanilla

6 servings

In 2-quart casserole, combine nectar, granulated sugar, brandy, water, cinnamon and ginger. Cover. Microwave at High for 3 to 5 minutes, or until mixture comes to a boil. Add peach slices. Stir to coat. Re-cover. Microwave at High for 5 to 6 minutes, or until peaches are tender, stirring once. Chill, covered, 30 minutes.

Drain and discard poaching liquid from peaches. Spoon peaches into individual serving dishes. In 4-cup measure, combine brown sugar and flour. Blend in cream and corn syrup. Mix well. Microwave at High for 2 to 3 minutes, or until mixture comes to a boil. Add margarine and vanilla, stirring until margarine is melted. Pour sauce evenly over peaches. Serve immediately.

*See How to Peel Apricots, page 74.

Per Serving: Calories: 230 • Protein: 1 g. • Carbohydrate: 33 g.
• Fat: 10 g. • Cholesterol: 22 mg. • Sodium: 61 mg.
Exchanges: ½ starch, 1¾ fruit, 2 fat

Strawberry-Rhubarb Custard

1 cup sliced rhubarb (¾-inch lengths)
¼ cup plus ⅓ cup sugar, divided
1 tablespoon all-purpose flour
1 cup sliced strawberries
¾ teaspoon cornstarch
⅛ teaspoon salt
2 cups milk
3 eggs, beaten
¾ teaspoon vanilla
    Boiling water

4 servings

In 1-quart casserole, combine rhubarb, ¼ cup sugar and the flour. Microwave at High for 3 to 4 minutes, or until rhubarb is tender-crisp. Stir in strawberries. Spoon mixture evenly into four 1⅓-cup custard cups. Set aside.

In small mixing bowl, combine remaining ⅓ cup sugar, the cornstarch and salt. Set aside. In 4-cup measure, microwave milk at High for 4 to 5 minutes, or until hot. Blend eggs and vanilla into sugar mixture. Beat egg mixture into hot milk.

Pour milk mixture evenly into custard cups. Place cups into 10-inch square casserole. Pour ½ inch boiling water into casserole around cups. Microwave at 50% (Medium) for 23 to 29 minutes, or until custard is set but still soft in center, rotating casserole ¼ turn every 3 minutes. Let stand for at least 30 minutes before serving. Serve warm or chilled.

Per Serving: Calories: 272 • Protein: 9 g. • Carbohydrate: 41 g.
• Fat: 8 g. • Cholesterol: 176 mg. • Sodium: 178 mg.
Exchanges: ¾ medium-fat meat, 2¼ fruit, ½ low-fat milk, 1 fat

Brownie Fruit Torte

1 pkg. (21½ oz.) fudge
　brownie mix
½ cup water
½ cup vegetable oil
1 egg

Filling:

1 pkg. (8 oz.) cream cheese,
　softened
½ cup powdered sugar

¼ cup whipping cream
½ teaspoon peppermint or
　almond extract

2 cups whole strawberries,
　hulled and cut lengthwise
　into quarters
2 kiwifruit, peeled and sliced
¾ cup red raspberries
　Fresh mint leaves (optional)

10 servings

Spray two 9-inch round cake dishes with nonstick vegetable cooking spray. Line bottom of each with wax paper. Set aside. In large mixing bowl, combine brownie mix, water, oil and egg.

Spread batter evenly in prepared dishes. Microwave one dish at 50% (Medium) for 6 minutes, rotating once. Microwave at High for 4 to 6 minutes longer, or until light and springy to the touch and no unbaked batter is visible through bottom of dish. Let stand on countertop for 10 minutes. Loosen edges and turn brownie layer out onto wire rack. Remove wax paper. Repeat with remaining dish. Cool completely.

In medium mixing bowl, combine filling ingredients. Beat at medium speed of electric mixer until mixture is smooth and creamy. Place 1 brownie layer on serving dish. Spread half of filling evenly on layer. Arrange half of fruit over filling. Repeat with remaining brownie layer, filling and fruit. Garnish with mint leaves. Refrigerate 1 to 2 hours before serving.

Per Serving: Calories: 513 • Protein: 5 g. • Carbohydrate: 65 g. • Fat: 26 g.
• Cholesterol: 53 mg. • Sodium: 305 mg.
Exchanges: 2 starch, 2¼ fruit, 5 fat

Summer Holiday ▲ Shortcake

3 cups red raspberries
⅓ cup plus ¼ cup sugar,
　divided
2 tablespoons crème de
　cassis
1 tablespoon cornstarch
　mixed with 1 tablespoon
　lemon juice
1¼ cups all-purpose flour
1 tablespoon baking powder
¼ teaspoon salt
¼ cup margarine or butter,
　cut into small pieces
¼ cup plain nonfat or low-fat
　yogurt
1 egg, beaten
2 teaspoons margarine or
　butter, melted
1½ cups blueberries, black
　raspberries or blackberries
¾ cup whipped cream

6 servings

Per Serving: Calories: 381 • Protein: 5 g.
• Carbohydrate: 56 g. • Fat: 15 g.
• Cholesterol: 52 mg. • Sodium: 433 mg.
Exchanges: 1¾ starch, 2 fruit, 3 fat

How to Microwave Summer Holiday Shortcake

Combine raspberries, 1/3 cup sugar and the crème de cassis in 2-quart casserole. Cover. Microwave at High for 3 to 4 minutes, or until sugar is dissolved, stirring once. In food processor or blender, blend until smooth.

Strain mixture through fine-mesh strainer into 4-cup measure, pressing with back of spoon to release juice. Discard seeds. Microwave juice at High for 2 to 4 minutes, or until very hot.

Stir in cornstarch mixture. Microwave at High for 1 to 1½ minutes, or until sauce is thickened and translucent, stirring every 30 seconds. Cool slightly. Cover with plastic wrap. Chill.

Spray 10-inch pie plate with nonstick vegetable cooking spray. Set aside. In medium mixing bowl, combine flour, remaining ¼ cup sugar, the baking powder and salt.

Add cut-up margarine. Beat at low speed of electric mixer until particles resemble coarse crumbs. Stir in yogurt and egg until particles are moistened and cling together.

Form dough into ball. Place on lightly floured surface. Form into circle. Roll dough to ½-inch thickness. Place in prepared plate. Brush with melted margarine. Microwave at High for 4 to 6 minutes, or until shortcake springs back when lightly touched in center and no unbaked dough is visible through bottom of plate.

Cool slightly. Spoon about ¼ cup raspberry sauce onto each serving plate. Place wedge of shortcake on each pool of sauce. Top wedges evenly with blueberries and whipped cream. For a decorative touch, place dots of yogurt in sauce around cake and drag wooden pick through middle of each.

Lemon-glazed Melons with Champagne ▼

- 2 cups honeydew melon balls (3/4-inch)
- 2 cups cantaloupe melon balls (3/4-inch)
- 2 cups seeded watermelon chunks (1-inch chunks)
- 1/2 cup sugar
- 1 tablespoon cornstarch
- 2 teaspoons grated lemon peel
- 1/3 cup water
- 3 tablespoons lemon juice
- 3 cups champagne or sparkling wine

6 servings

In large mixing bowl, combine melons. Set aside.

In 4-cup measure, combine sugar, cornstarch and peel. Blend in water and juice. Microwave at High for 3 to 3 1/2 minutes, or until mixture is thickened and translucent, stirring after 2 minutes and then every minute. Cool slightly. Pour over melons. Toss gently to coat. Cover. Chill 30 minutes.

Spoon melon mixture evenly into 6 serving bowls. Pour champagne evenly over melons. Garnish with blueberries and mint leaves, if desired. Serve immediately.

Per Serving: Calories: 212 • Protein: 1 g.
• Carbohydrate: 33 g. • Fat: 0
• Cholesterol: 0 • Sodium: 20 mg.
Exchanges: 2 fruit, 2 fat

Fresh Fruit Jelly Roll ▼

Jelly Roll:
- 3 eggs
- 1 cup granulated sugar
- 1/4 cup water
- 1 teaspoon almond extract
- 1 cup all-purpose flour
- 2 teaspoons baking powder
- 1/2 teaspoon salt

  Powdered sugar

Fruit Filling:
- 1/2 cup granulated sugar
- 2 tablespoons cornstarch
- 1 tablespoon all-purpose flour
- 1/8 teaspoon salt
- 2 cups milk
- 3 egg yolks
- 2 tablespoons margarine or butter
- 1 teaspoon almond extract
- 1 cup chopped pitted bing cherries
- 1 cup chopped peeled red pears
- 1 cup blueberries
- 1/4 cup slivered almonds, toasted, divided

  Whole bing cherries

10 servings

Per Serving: Calories: 315 • Protein: 7 g.
• Carbohydrate: 52 g. • Fat: 9 g.
• Cholesterol: 134 mg. • Sodium: 300 mg.
Exchanges: 1 starch, 1/2 medium-fat meat, 2 1/2 fruit, 1 1/4 fat

How to Make Fresh Fruit Jelly Roll

Heat conventional oven to 375°F. Grease and flour 15½ × 10½ × 1½-inch jelly roll pan. Set aside. In large mixing bowl, beat eggs at high speed of electric mixer until thick and lemon-colored (about 5 minutes). Gradually add 1 cup granulated sugar, beating until light and fluffy. Stir in water and almond extract.

Add remaining jelly roll ingredients. Beat at low speed of electric mixer just until moistened. Spread batter evenly in prepared pan.

Bake for 10 to 13 minutes, or until top springs back when lightly touched in center. Loosen edges. Immediately turn onto towel dusted with powdered sugar.

Roll up cake in towel, starting at narrow end. Cool completely on wire rack. Prepare fruit filling. In 2-quart casserole, combine sugar, cornstarch, flour and salt. Blend in milk. Microwave at High for 8 to 10 minutes, or until mixture thickens, stirring every 3 minutes. In small mixing bowl, beat egg yolks. Gradually stir in ½ cup hot mixture.

Blend egg yolk mixture back into hot mixture. Mix well. Microwave at High for 1 to 1½ minutes, or until mixture thickens, stirring once. Stir in margarine and almond extract.

Place plastic wrap directly on surface of mixture to prevent skin from forming. Chill 30 minutes. Fold fruits and 3 tablespoons almonds into mixture. Unroll cake; remove towel.

Spread fruit filling evenly on cake. Loosely reroll cake. Garnish with whole cherries and remaining 1 tablespoon almonds. Chill 1 hour before serving.

Rummed Fruit Meringues

Meringue:
1 cup powdered sugar
2 tablespoons cornstarch
1 teaspoon granulated sugar
½ teaspoon cocoa
4 egg whites
¼ teaspoon cream of tartar
¼ teaspoon vanilla

Sauce:

1 tablespoon granulated sugar
1 teaspoon cornstarch
¼ cup orange juice

2 tablespoons rum
2 teaspoons lemon juice

1½ cups coarsely chopped pineapple
1½ cups hulled and halved strawberries
2 kiwifruit, peeled, cut in half and sliced
1 cup blueberries

6 servings

Per Serving: Calories: 187 • Protein: 3 g. • Carbohydrate: 42 g.
• Fat: 1 g. • Cholesterol: 0 • Sodium: 41 mg.
Exchanges: ½ lean meat, 2¾ fruit

How to Make Rummed Fruit Meringues

Heat conventional oven to 250°F. Line baking sheet with parchment paper or sheet cut from brown paper bag. Draw six 3½-inch circles on paper.

Sift powdered sugar and 2 tablespoons cornstarch together into small mixing bowl. Set aside.

Combine 1 teaspoon granulated sugar and the cocoa in small bowl. Set aside. In large mixing bowl, combine remaining meringue ingredients.

Beat at high speed of electric mixer until soft peaks begin to form. Add powdered sugar mixture, 1 tablespoon at a time, while beating at high speed. Beat until mixture is thick and glossy.

Spoon mixture into pastry bag fitted with star tip, and pipe on circles on prepared baking sheet. Or use spoon to form circles, mounding slightly around edges.

Sprinkle meringues evenly with cocoa mixture. Bake for 2 hours. Turn oven off. (Do not open door.) Let meringues stand in oven for 1 hour.

Remove meringues from oven and cool to room temperature. Meanwhile, in 2-cup measure, combine 1 tablespoon granulated sugar and 1 teaspoon cornstarch.

Stir in remaining sauce ingredients. Microwave at High for 1 to 1½ minutes, or until sauce is thickened and translucent, stirring every minute. Chill.

Combine remaining ingredients in large mixing bowl. Spoon fruit mixture evenly into meringues. Drizzle sauce evenly over fruit. Top with whipped cream, if desired.

Kiwi-Honeydew Sorbet

  2 cups sugar
1½ cups water
  ¼ cup lemon juice
1½ cups cubed honeydew melon (½-inch
       cubes)
  3 kiwifruit, peeled and coarsely chopped

8 servings

In 8-cup measure, combine sugar, water and
juice. Microwave at High for 4 to 6 minutes, or
until sugar is dissolved, stirring once. Set aside.

In food processor or blender, combine melon
and kiwifruit. Process until smooth (about 2 cups).
Add to sugar mixture. Stir to combine. Pour mixture into 12 × 8-inch baking dish. Freeze 4 to 6
hours, or until firm, stirring once every hour to
break apart. Cover with plastic wrap and freeze
overnight, if desired.

Let sorbet stand at room temperature for 5 to 10
minutes to soften before serving, if necessary.

Per Serving: Calories: 223 • Protein: 0 • Carbohydrate: 57 g.
• Fat: 0 • Cholesterol: 0 • Sodium: 7 mg.
Exchanges: 3¾ fruit

Ginger-Szechuan Nectarine Ice

  1 cup hot water
  ½ cup sugar
  ⅛ teaspoon crushed red pepper flakes
  4 medium nectarines, peeled
  2 tablespoons finely chopped peeled fresh
       gingerroot
  ½ cup vanilla-flavored low-fat yogurt

6 servings

In 4-cup measure, combine water, sugar and
red pepper flakes. Microwave at High for 1 to 2
minutes, or until sugar is dissolved, stirring once.
Set aside.

Pit and slice nectarines over medium mixing
bowl to catch any juice. In food processor or
blender, combine nectarine slices, juice and
gingerroot. Process until smooth (about 2 cups).
Add to sugar mixture. Stir to combine. Pour mixture into 9-inch round cake dish. Freeze 4 to 6
hours, or until firm, stirring once every hour to
break apart. Cover with plastic wrap and freeze
overnight, if desired.

Let nectarine ice stand at room temperature for
5 to 10 minutes to soften, if necessary. Place
in food processor or blender. Add yogurt. Process until smooth. Return to cake dish. Freeze
until firm.

Per Serving: Calories: 126 • Protein: 2 g. • Carbohydrate: 30 g.
• Fat: 1 g. • Cholesterol: 1 mg. • Sodium: 13 mg.
Exchanges: 2 fruit

Mango-Mint Sorbet

     2 cups sugar
  1½ cups water
     ¼ cup lemon juice
     ¼ cup snipped fresh mint leaves
     2 mangos, peeled and coarsely chopped

8 servings

In 8-cup measure, combine sugar, water, juice and mint leaves. Microwave at High for 4 to 6 minutes, or until sugar is dissolved, stirring once. Let stand for 5 minutes (longer for stronger mint flavor). Strain mixture through fine-mesh strainer. Discard mint leaves. Set mixture aside.

In food processor or blender, process mangos until smooth (about 2 cups). Add to sugar mixture. Stir to combine. Pour mixture into 12 × 8-inch baking dish. Freeze 4 to 6 hours, or until firm, stirring once every hour to break apart. Cover with plastic wrap and freeze overnight, if desired.

Let sorbet stand at room temperature for 5 to 10 minutes to soften before serving, if necessary. Garnish with additional mint leaves or crushed peppermint candy, if desired.

Per Serving: Calories: 228 • Protein: 0 • Carbohydrate: 59 g. • Fat: 0 • Cholesterol: 0 • Sodium: 3 mg.
Exchanges: 4 fruit

Peach Sorbet

  1½ cups sugar
  1¼ cups water
     ¼ cup lime juice
     3 medium peaches, pitted and coarsely chopped

8 servings

In 8-cup measure, combine sugar, water and juice. Microwave at High for 4 to 6 minutes, or until sugar is dissolved, stirring once. Set aside.

In food processor or blender, process peaches until smooth (about 2½ cups). Add to sugar mixture. Stir to combine. Pour mixture into 12 × 8-inch baking dish. Freeze 4 to 6 hours, or until firm, stirring once every hour to break apart. Cover with plastic wrap and freeze overnight, if desired.

Let sorbet stand at room temperature for 5 to 10 minutes to soften before serving, if necessary.

Per Serving: Calories: 167 • Protein: 0 • Carbohydrate: 43 g. • Fat: 0 • Cholesterol: 0 • Sodium: 2 mg.
Exchanges: 2¾ fruit

Apricot-Banana Freeze

1 cup red raspberries
1/2 cup plus 3 tablespoons granulated sugar, divided
1 teaspoon cornstarch mixed with 2 teaspoons water
4 medium apricots, pitted and quartered
1/4 cup orange juice
1 cup quick-cooking oats
1/4 cup slivered almonds
1/2 cup packed brown sugar
1/3 cup margarine or butter, softened
3/4 teaspoon ground allspice
1/2 cup nonfat dry milk powder
2 egg whites
1 medium banana, peeled and sliced

6 to 8 servings

In small mixing bowl, combine raspberries and 3 tablespoons granulated sugar. Microwave at High for 2 to 3 minutes, or until sugar is dissolved. Strain mixture through fine-mesh strainer into 2-cup measure, pressing with back of spoon to release juice. Discard seeds. Microwave juice at High for 1 to 1 1/2 minutes, or until very hot. Stir in cornstarch mixture. Microwave at High for 30 to 45 seconds, or until sauce is thickened and translucent, stirring every 30 seconds. Cool slightly. Cover with plastic wrap. Chill.

In 1 1/2-quart casserole, combine apricots and juice. Cover. Microwave at High for 5 to 6 minutes, or until apricots are tender, stirring once. In food processor or blender, process mixture until smooth. Pour into large mixing bowl. Stir in 1/4 cup sugar. Chill.

Heat conventional oven to 350°F. Spread oats in shallow pan. Bake for 5 minutes. Stir in almonds. Bake for additional 8 to 10 minutes, or until golden brown, stirring once or twice. In medium mixing bowl, combine oat mixture, brown sugar, margarine and allspice. Press mixture into bottom of 8-inch square baking dish. Chill.

To apricot mixture, add milk powder and egg whites. Beat at high speed of electric mixer until light and foamy. Gradually beat in remaining 1/4 cup sugar. Fold in banana. Pour mixture into prepared baking dish.

Drizzle raspberry sauce in horizontal lines over filling. Marble by dragging knife vertically through sauce lines. Freeze at least 4 hours, or until firm. Let stand at room temperature for 5 to 10 minutes to soften before serving, if necessary.

Per Serving: Calories: 302 • Protein: 5 g. • Carbohydrate: 49 g. • Fat: 11 g.
• Cholesterol: 1 mg. • Sodium: 131 mg.
Exchanges: 1 starch, 2 fruit, 1/4 low-fat milk, 2 fat

Banana-Mango Salsa

⅓ cup packed brown sugar
2½ teaspoons cornstarch
¾ cup unsweetened
    pineapple juice
2 tablespoons margarine or
    butter, melted
2 medium bananas, peeled
    and sliced
1 mango, peeled and
    coarsely chopped

8 servings

In 1½-quart casserole, combine sugar and cornstarch. Blend in juice and margarine. Microwave at High for 4 to 6 minutes, or until mixture is thickened and translucent, stirring once. Stir in remaining ingredients. Serve salsa warm over ice cream. Garnish with toasted fresh coconut curls (page 127), if desired.

Variation: Substitute 2 medium plums, pitted and coarsely chopped, for one banana.

Per Serving: Calories: 119 • Protein: 1 g.
• Carbohydrate: 24 g. • Fat: 3 g.
• Cholesterol: 0 • Sodium: 37 mg.
Exchanges: 1½ fruit, ½ fat

Cinnamon Chips with Crenshaw Salsa ▲

¼ cup plus 2 tablespoons
    sugar, divided
2 teaspoons cornstarch
1 teaspoon grated lemon peel
½ cup water
1 tablespoon lemon juice
3 cups finely chopped
    Crenshaw melon
1 teaspoon ground cinnamon
6 flour tortillas (8-inch)
2 tablespoons margarine or
    butter, melted
    Red cinnamon candies
    (optional)

6 to 8 servings

In 2-cup measure, combine ¼ cup sugar, the cornstarch and peel. Blend in water and juice. Microwave at High for 2½ to 3 minutes, or until mixture is thickened and translucent, stirring every minute. In medium mixing bowl, combine lemon mixture and melon. Chill salsa.

In small bowl, combine remaining 2 tablespoons sugar and the cinnamon. Brush tortillas evenly with margarine. Sprinkle with cinnamon and sugar mixture. Cut each tortilla into 6 wedges.

On paper-towel-lined plate, arrange 12 wedges, slightly overlapping. Microwave at High for 4 to 5 minutes, or until crisp, rotating plate once. Loosen chips from paper towel immediately. Set aside.

Repeat with remaining tortilla wedges. Garnish salsa with cinnamon candies. Serve chips with salsa.

Per Serving: Calories: 172 • Protein: 3 g. • Carbohydrate: 33 g. • Fat: 3 g.
• Cholesterol: 0 • Sodium: 196 mg.
Exchanges: 1¼ starch, 1 fruit, ½ fat

Stuffed Apples ▲

4 medium red or green cooking apples
1/4 cup carbonated water
1 tablespoon lemon juice
1/4 teaspoon ground allspice

Stuffing:
3 oz. cream cheese, softened
2 tablespoons finely chopped pecans,
 walnuts or hazelnuts
1 teaspoon sugar
1 teaspoon grated orange peel

4 servings

Core apples to within 1/2 inch of bottom. Place in four 1 1/3-cup custard cups. In 1-cup measure, combine carbonated water, juice and allspice. Pour mixture evenly into apples. Cover loosely with plastic wrap. Microwave at High for 7 to 11 minutes, or until apples are tender, rotating and rearranging once. Drain apples.

Meanwhile, combine stuffing ingredients. Spoon stuffing evenly into apples. Re-cover. Let stand for 2 minutes. Serve warm.

Variation 1: Prepare as directed, except substitute 1/2 cup crumbled blue cheese for cream cheese and omit sugar and peel.

Variation 2: Prepare as directed, except substitute medium d'Anjou pears for apples. Microwave pears at High for 5 to 8 minutes, or until tender.

Per Serving: Calories: 175 • Protein: 2 g. • Carbohydrate: 24 g. • Fat: 9 g. • Cholesterol: 21 mg. • Sodium: 56 mg. Exchanges: 1 1/2 fruit, 2 fat

Fruited Floating Island

2 1/2 cups hot water, divided
2/3 cup sugar, divided
1 tablespoon lemon juice
4 cups coarsely chopped seeded yellow
 watermelon
4 egg whites
1/2 teaspoon grated lemon peel
 Blueberries or small strawberries (optional)

4 servings

In 2-cup measure, combine 1/2 cup water, 1/3 cup sugar and the juice. Microwave at High for 1 1/2 to 2 minutes, or until sugar is dissolved. In food processor or blender, combine sugar mixture and watermelon. Process until smooth (about 3 1/2 cups). Chill.

In medium mixing bowl, beat egg whites at high speed of electric mixer until soft peaks begin to form. Gradually beat in remaining 1/3 cup sugar until stiff peaks form. Beat in peel. Set aside.

Pour remaining 2 cups water into 10-inch square casserole. Cover. Microwave at High for 6 to 8 minutes, or until very hot. Using 2 large spoons, scoop out one-fourth of egg white mixture and drop into steaming water. Repeat with remaining mixture. Cover. Microwave at 50% (Medium) for 3 to 5 minutes, or just until meringues feel firm, rotating dish once.

Using slotted spatula, remove meringues. Drain on paper-towel-lined plate. Chill. To serve, pour watermelon mixture into serving dishes. Float 1 meringue in each dish. Sprinkle blueberries into dishes around meringues. Garnish with additional peel, if desired.

Per Serving: Calories: 198 • Protein: 5 g. • Carbohydrate: 45 g. • Fat: 1 g. • Cholesterol: 0 • Sodium: 59 mg. Exchanges: 1/2 lean meat, 3 fruit

Zucchini Chip Bread

1 1/4 cups all-purpose flour
1 medium zucchini,
    shredded (1 cup)
1/2 cup packed brown sugar
1/3 cup margarine or butter,
    softened
2 eggs
1/4 cup milk
1 teaspoon baking soda
1/2 teaspoon salt
1/2 cup miniature semisweet
    chocolate chips

16 servings

Per Serving: Calories: 132 • Protein: 2 g.
• Carbohydrate: 18 g. • Fat: 6 g.
• Cholesterol: 27 mg. • Sodium: 176 mg.
Exchanges: 1 starch, 1/4 fruit, 1 1/4 fat

How to Microwave Zucchini Chip Bread

Line bottom of 8 x 4-inch loaf dish with wax paper. Set aside. In large mixing bowl, combine all ingredients, except chocolate chips.

Beat at low speed of electric mixer until combined. Beat at medium speed for 2 minutes. Stir in chips. Spread batter in prepared dish.

Shield ends of loaf with 2-inch-wide strips of foil, covering 1 inch of batter and molding remainder around handles of dish.

Center dish on saucer in oven. Microwave at 50% (Medium) for 9 minutes, rotating dish 1/4 turn every 3 minutes.

Remove foil. Microwave at High for 3 to 6 minutes, or until no unbaked batter is visible through bottom of dish, rotating every 2 minutes.

Let stand for 10 minutes. Loosen edges and turn loaf out onto wire rack. Remove wax paper. Cool completely before slicing.

Sour Cream Potato Muffins

1 medium russet potato, peeled and cut into 1/2-inch cubes (1 cup)
1/4 cup water
1 1/4 cups all-purpose flour
2 tablespoons sugar
1 teaspoon baking powder
1/2 teaspoon baking soda
1/4 teaspoon salt
2/3 cup sour cream
1 egg
1 tablespoon snipped fresh chives
2 teaspoons sesame seed, toasted, divided

1 dozen muffins

Line microwave cupcake dish with 2 paper liners per cup. Set aside. In 1 1/2-quart casserole, combine potato and water. Cover. Microwave at High for 5 to 6 minutes, or until potato is tender, stirring once. Mash potato and water until smooth. Stir in enough additional water to equal 1 1/4 cups. Set aside.

In large mixing bowl, combine flour, sugar, baking powder, baking soda and salt. Add sour cream, egg and chives to potato mixture. Mix well. Add to flour mixture. Stir just until moistened. Fill prepared cups about half full. Set remaining batter aside.

Sprinkle tops evenly with 1 teaspoon sesame seed. Microwave at High for 4 to 5 minutes, or until light and springy to the touch, rotating dish once. (Some moist areas may remain on top surface, but will dry during standing.) Let stand for 2 minutes. Remove muffins to wire rack to cool slightly. Repeat with remaining batter and 1 teaspoon sesame seed. Serve warm.

Per Serving: Calories: 103 • Protein: 3 g.
• Carbohydrate: 15 g. • Fat: 3 g.
• Cholesterol: 23 mg. • Sodium: 128 mg.
Exchanges: 1 starch, 3/4 fat

Strawberry Corn Muffins ▲

2 pkgs. (7 oz. each) cornmeal muffin mix
1 tablespoon granulated sugar
2/3 cup milk
1 egg
1 cup chopped strawberries
Powdered sugar (optional)

1 dozen muffins

Line microwave cupcake dish with 2 paper liners per cup. Set aside. In large mixing bowl, combine muffin mix and granulated sugar. Add milk and egg. Stir until well blended. Fold in strawberries. Fill prepared cups about two-thirds full. Set remaining batter aside.

Microwave at High for 3 to 5 minutes, or until light and springy to the touch, rotating dish once. (Some moist areas may remain on top surface, but will dry during standing.) Let stand for 2 minutes. Remove muffins to wire rack to cool slightly. Repeat with remaining batter. Dust muffin tops with powdered sugar. Serve warm.

Per Serving: Calories: 192 • Protein: 4 g. • Carbohydrate: 32 g. • Fat: 5 g.
• Cholesterol: 20 mg. • Sodium: 310 mg.
Exchanges: 2 starch, 1 fat

Carrot Apricot Muffins

1½ cups all-purpose flour
½ cup quick-cooking oats
½ cup shredded carrot
⅓ cup snipped dried apricots
⅓ cup chopped walnuts
¼ cup golden raisins
¼ cup packed brown sugar
2 teaspoons baking powder
1 teaspoon ground
   cinnamon, divided
¼ teaspoon salt
⅛ teaspoon ground nutmeg
1 cup milk
1 egg
¼ cup vegetable oil
1 tablespoon plus 1½
   teaspoons granulated
   sugar

1 dozen muffins

Line microwave cupcake dish with 2 paper liners per cup. Set aside. In large mixing bowl, combine flour, oats, carrot, apricots, walnuts, raisins, brown sugar, baking powder, ¾ teaspoon cinnamon, the salt and nutmeg. Add milk, egg and oil. Stir just until moistened. Fill prepared cups about two-thirds full. Set remaining batter aside.

Microwave at High for 3 to 5 minutes, or until light and springy to the touch, rotating dish once. (Some moist areas may remain on top surface, but will dry during standing.) Let stand for 2 minutes. Remove muffins to wire rack to cool slightly. Repeat with remaining batter. In small bowl, combine granulated sugar and remaining ¼ teaspoon cinnamon. Sprinkle evenly over muffin tops. Serve warm.

Per Serving: Calories: 194 • Protein: 4 g.
• Carbohydrate: 27 g. • Fat: 8 g.
• Cholesterol: 21 mg. • Sodium: 136 mg.
Exchanges: 1 starch, ¾ fruit, 1¾ fat

Pear Bran Muffins ▲

1 cup bran flakes cereal
½ cup milk
1 cup all-purpose flour
2 tablespoons packed
   brown sugar
1½ teaspoons baking powder
1 teaspoon grated lemon
   peel
¼ teaspoon ground allspice
¼ teaspoon salt
1 medium red pear, cored
   and chopped
¼ cup vegetable oil
¼ cup honey
1 egg, beaten

1 dozen muffins

In small mixing bowl, combine cereal and milk. Let stand for 15 minutes, or until cereal is soft, stirring occasionally. Line microwave cupcake dish with 2 paper liners per cup. Set aside. In large mixing bowl, combine flour, sugar, baking powder, peel, allspice and salt. Add cereal mixture and remaining ingredients. Stir just until moistened. Fill prepared cups about half full. Set remaining batter aside.

Sprinkle tops with crushed bran flakes, if desired. Microwave at High for 5 to 7 minutes, or until light and springy to the touch, rotating dish once. (Some moist areas may remain on top surface, but will dry during standing.) Let stand for 2 minutes. Remove muffins to wire rack to cool slightly. Repeat with remaining batter. Serve warm.

Per Serving: Calories: 140 • Protein: 2 g. • Carbohydrate: 21 g. • Fat: 5 g.
• Cholesterol: 19 mg. • Sodium: 140 mg.
Exchanges: 1 starch, ½ fruit, 1 fat

Fig Bread

  1 lb. Black Mission figs
       (15 to 18), peeled and
       chopped
  2 cups all-purpose flour
 1/3 cup packed brown sugar
1 1/2 teaspoons baking powder
1 1/2 teaspoons grated fresh
       gingerroot
 1/2 teaspoon salt
 1/2 cup chopped dried figs or
       raisins
 1/3 cup milk
 1/4 cup vegetable oil
  1 egg
  2 tablespoons finely
       chopped walnuts or
       pecans

16 servings

Line bottom of 8 × 4-inch loaf dish with wax paper. Set aside. In food processor or blender, process figs until smooth (about 1 cup). Set aside. In large mixing bowl, combine flour, sugar, baking powder, gingerroot and salt. Set aside.

In medium mixing bowl, combine puréed figs and remaining ingredients, except walnuts. Beat at low speed of electric mixer until blended. Add to flour mixture. Mix well. Spread batter in prepared dish. Sprinkle walnuts on top.

Shield ends of loaf with 2-inch-wide strips of foil, covering 1 inch of batter and molding remainder around handles of dish. Center dish on saucer in oven. Microwave at 50% (Medium) for 9 minutes, rotating dish 1/4 turn every 3 minutes. Remove foil. Microwave at High for 8 to 10 minutes, or until no unbaked batter is visible through bottom of dish, rotating every 2 minutes. Let stand for 10 minutes. Loosen edges and turn loaf out onto wire rack. Remove wax paper. Cool completely before slicing.

Per Serving: Calories: 155 • Protein: 3 g.
• Carbohydrate: 26 g. • Fat: 5 g.
• Cholesterol: 14 mg. • Sodium: 117 mg.
Exchanges: 3/4 starch, 1 fruit, 1 fat

Hot Peppered Corn Bread ▲

 1 cup all-purpose flour
 1 cup yellow cornmeal
 1 tablespoon sugar
 1 tablespoon baking powder
 1 teaspoon ground cumin
1/2 teaspoon salt
 2 ears corn on the cob (8 to
    10 oz. each), kernels sliced
    off (1 1/2 cups) and cobs
    discarded

 2 eggs, beaten
1/2 cup milk
1/3 cup vegetable oil
 1 jalapeño pepper, sliced
    and seeded
 1 red chili pepper, sliced and
    seeded

8 servings

Spray 9-inch round cake dish with nonstick vegetable cooking spray. Set aside. In medium mixing bowl, combine flour, cornmeal, sugar, baking powder, cumin and salt. Stir in remaining ingredients, reserving half of pepper slices.

Spread cornmeal mixture in prepared dish. Arrange reserved pepper slices on top. Sprinkle with paprika, if desired. Center dish on saucer in oven. Microwave at 50% (Medium) for 6 minutes, rotating once. Microwave at High for 4 to 5 minutes, or until no unbaked batter is visible through bottom of dish, rotating every 2 minutes. Let stand for 10 minutes. Serve with honey or honey-butter spread, if desired.

Per Serving: Calories: 267 • Protein: 6 g. • Carbohydrate: 35 g. • Fat: 12 g.
• Cholesterol: 55 mg. • Sodium: 326 mg.
Exchanges: 2 1/4 starch, 2 1/4 fat

Onion & Gorgonzola Focaccia

1 medium red onion, cut into ¼-inch slices
1 medium Vidalia onion, cut into ¼-inch slices
2 tablespoons olive oil
1 tablespoon snipped fresh rosemary leaves
2 cloves garlic, minced
1 pkg. (16 oz.) hot roll mix
1¼ cups hot water (120 to 130°F)
2 tablespoons vegetable oil
½ cup plus 2 tablespoons crumbled Gorgonzola cheese, divided

8 to 10 servings

Per Serving: Calories: 242 • Protein: 7 g.
• Carbohydrate: 35 g. • Fat: 9 g.
• Cholesterol: 6 mg. • Sodium: 414 mg.
Exchanges: 2 starch, ½ high-fat meat, ½ vegetable, 1 fat

Spray 12-inch round pizza pan or large baking sheet with nonstick vegetable cooking spray. Set aside. In 10-inch square casserole, combine onions, olive oil, rosemary and garlic. Cover. Microwave at High for 6 to 7 minutes, or until onions are tender-crisp, stirring once. Set aside.

In large mixing bowl, combine hot roll mix, water and vegetable oil. Turn dough out onto lightly floured surface. Shape into ball. Knead for 5 minutes, or until smooth. Split dough in half. Press half of dough into 11-inch circle. Place circle on prepared pan. Spoon half of onion mixture onto dough circle, spreading to within 1 inch of edge. Sprinkle evenly with ½ cup cheese.

Press second half of dough into 11-inch circle. Fit second circle over filling, pressing edges to seal. Heat conventional oven to 375°F. Cover focaccia with cloth. Let rise in warm place for 10 to 15 minutes, or until focaccia is doubled in size and impressions remain in dough when pressed with 2 fingers to about ½-inch depth. Indent dough randomly with fingertips. Top with remaining onion mixture and 2 tablespoons cheese. Bake for 22 to 25 minutes, or until golden brown. Serve warm in wedges.

Leek & Sweet Pepper Garlic Braid ▶

 1 cup thinly sliced leeks
 1 cup chopped red pepper
1/4 cup margarine or butter, softened, divided
 2 large cloves garlic, minced
1/4 teaspoon salt
1/4 teaspoon freshly ground pepper
 1 pkg. (16 oz.) hot roll mix
1/2 teaspoon garlic powder
 1 cup hot water (120 to 130°F)
 1 egg
 1 egg white
 1 teaspoon water
 1 tablespoon grated Parmesan cheese

8 to 10 servings

Spray large baking sheet with nonstick vegetable cooking spray. Set aside. In 1 1/2-quart casserole, combine leeks, red pepper, 2 tablespoons margarine, the garlic, salt and pepper. Cover. Microwave at High for 3 to 5 minutes, or until vegetables are tender-crisp, stirring once. Set aside.

In large mixing bowl, combine hot roll mix, garlic powder, remaining 2 tablespoons margarine, the hot water and egg. Form dough into ball. Place on lightly floured surface. Knead for 5 minutes, or until smooth.

Roll dough into 14 × 11-inch rectangle. Place on prepared baking sheet. Spread leek mixture down center third of rectangle to within 1 inch of short ends.

Fold short ends of dough 1 inch over filling; pinch to seal. Along long sides, make cuts at 1-inch intervals, cutting from edge to within 1/2 inch of filling. Fold strips diagonally over filling, alternating from side to side. Fold ends of strips under to seal.

Heat conventional oven to 375°F. Cover braid with cloth. Let rise in warm place for 20 to 30 minutes, or until braid is doubled in size.

In small bowl, beat egg white and water. Brush braid with egg wash. Sprinkle with Parmesan cheese. Bake for 20 to 23 minutes, or until golden brown. Serve warm in slices.

Per Serving: Calories: 214 • Protein: 6 g. • Carbohydrate: 34 g. • Fat: 6 g. • Cholesterol: 22 mg. • Sodium: 424 mg.
Exchanges: 2 1/4 starch, 1/4 vegetable, 1 fat

Mediterranean Spinach & Feta Bread ▶

1/2 cup chopped red onion
 2 tablespoons olive oil
 2 large cloves garlic, minced
1/2 teaspoon dried oregano leaves
1/4 teaspoon freshly ground pepper
 8 cups torn spinach leaves
 1 pkg. (16 oz.) hot roll mix
1/4 teaspoon garlic powder
 1 cup hot water (120 to 130°F)
 1 egg
 2 tablespoons margarine or butter, softened
1/2 cup plus 2 tablespoons crumbled feta cheese, divided
   Kalamata (Greek) olives (optional)

8 to 10 servings

Spray 12-inch round pizza pan or large baking sheet with nonstick vegetable cooking spray. Set aside. In 3-quart casserole, combine onion, oil, garlic, oregano and pepper. Cover. Microwave at High for 3 to 4 minutes, or until onion is tender-crisp, stirring once. Add spinach. Mix well. Re-cover. Microwave at High for 2 to 2 1/2 minutes, or until spinach just begins to wilt. Set aside.

In large mixing bowl, combine hot roll mix, garlic powder, water, egg and margarine. Form dough into ball. Place on lightly floured surface. Knead for 5 minutes, or until smooth. Split dough in half. Press half of dough into 11-inch circle. Place circle on prepared pan. Spoon half of spinach mixture onto circle, spreading to within 1 inch of edge. Sprinkle evenly with 1/2 cup cheese.

Press second half of dough into 11-inch circle. Fit second circle over filling, pressing edges to seal. Heat conventional oven to 375°F. Cover bread with cloth. Let rise in warm place for 20 to 30 minutes, or until bread is doubled in size and impressions remain when dough is pressed with 2 fingers to about 1/2-inch depth. Indent dough randomly with fingertips.

Top with remaining spinach mixture and 2 tablespoons cheese. Bake for 22 to 25 minutes, or until golden brown. Garnish with olives. Serve warm in wedges.

Per Serving: Calories: 240 • Protein: 8 g. • Carbohydrate: 35 g. • Fat: 8 g. • Cholesterol: 29 mg. • Sodium: 457 mg.
Exchanges: 1 3/4 starch, 1 1/2 vegetable, 1 3/4 fat

Chinese Stuffed Buns

Filling:

- ½ cup chopped enoki mushrooms
- ½ cup diagonally sliced snow pea pods (1-inch lengths)
- ⅓ cup thinly sliced leek
- ⅓ cup finely chopped red pepper
- 2 tablespoons soy sauce
- 2 teaspoons vegetable oil
- 1 teaspoon sugar
- 1 teaspoon grated fresh gingerroot
- 1 clove garlic, minced
- 1 teaspoon cornstarch mixed with 1 teaspoon water

- 1 pkg. (16 oz.) hot roll mix
- 1 cup hot water (120 to 130°F)
- 1 egg
- 2 tablespoons margarine or butter, softened
- 1 egg white, beaten with 1 tablespoon water
- 1 tablespoon sesame seed

1 dozen buns

Spray large baking sheet with nonstick vegetable cooking spray. Set aside. In 1½-quart casserole, combine all filling ingredients, except cornstarch mixture. Cover. Microwave at High for 3 to 4 minutes, or until pea pods brighten in color and mixture is hot, stirring once. Stir in cornstarch mixture. Microwave at High for 30 seconds to 1 minute, or until mixture is thickened and translucent, stirring once. Set aside.

In large mixing bowl, combine hot roll mix, water, egg and margarine. Form dough into ball. Place on lightly floured surface. Knead for 5 minutes, or until smooth.

Divide dough into 12 equal pieces. Shape into balls. Roll out 1 ball into 4-inch circle. Place heaping tablespoon filling in center. Pull edges over filling, pinching to seal. Repeat with remaining dough and filling. Arrange buns seam-side-down on prepared baking sheet. Cover with cloth. Heat conventional oven to 375°F. Let buns rise in warm place for 20 to 30 minutes, or until doubled in size.

Brush tops of buns with egg white mixture. Sprinkle evenly with sesame seed. Bake conventionally for 15 to 18 minutes, or until golden brown. Serve immediately.

Per Serving: Calories: 171 • Protein: 5 g. • Carbohydrate: 28 g. • Fat: 4 g.
• Cholesterol: 18 mg. • Sodium: 449 mg.
Exchanges: 1¾ starch, ½ vegetable, ¾ fat

Herbed Bruschetta ▲

- 1 small clove garlic, minced
- ¼ cup olive oil, divided
- ¼ teaspoon paprika
- ¼ teaspoon freshly ground pepper
- ⅛ to ¼ teaspoon salt
- 1 tablespoon snipped fresh oregano leaves
- 6 slices (1 inch thick) French bread, toasted
- ¼ cup plus 2 tablespoons shredded fresh Parmesan cheese

6 servings

In 1-cup measure, combine garlic and 1 teaspoon oil. Microwave at High for 1 to 1½ minutes, or until garlic is tender, stirring once. Stir in remaining 3 tablespoons plus 2 teaspoons oil, the paprika, pepper and salt. Microwave at High for 1 to 1½ minutes, or until hot. Stir in oregano. Sprinkle each slice of toast with 1 tablespoon Parmesan cheese. Drizzle oil mixture evenly over each slice. Serve immediately.

Per Serving: Calories: 210 • Protein: 6 g.
• Carbohydrate: 20 g. • Fat: 12 g.
• Cholesterol: 6 mg. • Sodium: 385 mg.
Exchanges: 1 ¼ starch, ¼ high-fat meat, 1¾ fat

Savory Lemon Rolls

- 1 pkg. (16 oz.) hot roll mix
- 2 tablespoons grated lemon peel
- 1 tablespoon snipped fresh rosemary leaves
- 1 cup hot water (120 to 130°F)
- ¼ cup margarine or butter, softened, divided
- 1 egg
- ½ cup shredded fresh Parmesan cheese
- 1 tablespoon poppy seed

1 dozen rolls

Spray two 10-inch pie plates with nonstick vegetable cooking spray. Set aside. In large mixing bowl, combine hot roll mix, peel and rosemary. Stir in water, 2 tablespoons margarine and the egg. Form dough into ball. Place on lightly floured surface. Knead for 5 minutes, or until smooth. Set aside.

In small mixing bowl, microwave remaining 2 tablespoons margarine at High for 30 to 45 seconds, or until melted. Set aside. In shallow dish, combine Parmesan cheese and poppy seed. Set aside.

Divide dough into 24 equal pieces. Shape into balls. Dip each ball in melted margarine and then roll in cheese mixture to coat. Place 9 rolls around edge and 3 rolls in center of each prepared plate. Cover with cloth. Let rolls rise in warm place for 20 to 30 minutes, or until doubled in size.

Microwave 1 plate at 50% (Medium) for 8 to 11 minutes, or until rolls spring back when touched, rotating ¼ turn every 2 minutes. Let stand for 5 minutes.

Remove rolls to wire rack to cool. Repeat with remaining plate. If desired, broil finished rolls conventionally 4 to 6 inches from heat for 5 to 7 minutes, or until golden brown.

Per Serving: Calories: 95 • Protein: 3 g. • Carbohydrate: 13 g. • Fat: 3 g.
• Cholesterol: 10 mg. • Sodium: 185 mg.
Exchanges: 1 starch, ⅔ fat

Index

Cy DeCosse Incorporated offers
Microwave Cooking Accessories
at special subscriber discounts.
For information write:

      Microwave Accessories
      5900 Green Oak Drive
      Minnetonka, MN 55343